RUNNING HOME

Day 1: "I liked the short intervals because they allowed me to rest in between..."

Day 10: "The chart is on the wall. We are becoming a running family. Jill did her workout running to school..."

Day 30: "There are days of relief, days of fear, days of soreness..."

Day 42: "We are more together, as our shoes get that worn feeling. I feel like another person. And that other person is a lot lighter in the world..."

from THE SIX-WEEK
TRAINING PROGRAM DIARY

Michael Spino's RUNNING HOME is a total fitness program for the entire family. It will *not* make an Olympic athlete out of you.

All it will do is change your life.

And your family.

For the better.

RUNNING HOME

**Introduction by
George Leonard**

A BERKLEY BOOK
published by
BERKLEY PUBLISHING CORPORATION

Celestial Arts
231 Adrian Road
Millbrae, California 94030

SBN 425-04005-4

BERKLEY MEDALLION BOOKS are published by
Berkley Publishing Corporation
200 Madison Avenue
New York, N.Y. 10016

BERKLEY BOOK ® TM 757,375

Printed in the United States of America

Berkley Edition, NOVEMBER, 1978

Dedication

To my wife, Judith,
and a visualized distant star,
to whom I am ever running home

Contents

Introduction

Some people run to reduce their waistlines or firm up their thighs, while others run to mend a damaged heart or strengthen a good one. Some people run to win at any cost, others to play the fine edge of potential and pain. Some run for altered consciousness, others just for the fun of it. And now—the damnedest thing!—millions of people are starting to run because it's *fashionable*. "Nowadays," declares a feature article in the society pages, "you're not really In unless you've run a marathon."

Whatever your reason for running, whether you run in sneakers and cutoffs or in the latest high-fashion jogging outfits, whether you run with the angels of enlightenment or the demons of hot competition, Mike Spino is your man. This Spino is not your crew-cut-stopwatch-clipboard kind of coach, nor is *Running Home* your run-of-the-mill running book. In fact, you'll probably never read another book on the subject that even faintly resembles this one. In it you'll find plenty of runner's lore: gaits, stretches, breathing techniques, tips on nutrition, an innovative six-week training program for runners at various levels. Then there's Spino's special gift to jaundiced pavement pounders: instructions on meditation and visualization, energy awareness and Feldenkrais movements, a whole array of Esalen body/mind/spirit disciplines tuned to the art of running.

But that's not all. As you jog or race your way through this book, you'll suddenly find yourself face to face with a Mike Spino stripped bare of his coach's mantle, his hard-won expertise. In poems and revelatory narratives, he reveals his fears and frustration and rage, and the moments of glorious madness that all human beings, and especially runners, are heir to. Once after an auto accident, Spino tells us, he was put under a spell by a sinister individual who appeared at the scene of the wreck. His account of this bizarre episode, in which he struggles mentally and finally physically for his freedom, evokes images of Castaneda's Indian sorceror, Don Juan.

What do these confessions of a passionate heart have to do with running? Not less than everything. Running ranks with the most primal of human acts, subsuming all mammalian evolution, preceding speech and even consciousness. Make no mistake about it, when you start to run or change your way of running, your whole life is likely to be transformed. If you're willing to run as Spino suggests for six weeks or more, you'll emerge a different animal. Your metabolism, that basic process through which digestion and respiration and blood flow are joined, will be significantly altered. Your appetitive regulator will be more finely tuned, your resting heartbeat slowed, your ability to handle stress enhanced. And as the constriction of your lungs and arteries is freed, so will be your thoughts and actions. It is life and all its possibilities that will flood in, and you should be prepared (especially if you're new to the game) for unfamiliar and sometimes frightening intensities of feeling where there might have been numbness, vivid colors in place of the gray, and perhaps a lovely and painful sense of how few years are left in which to run. *Bon Voyage!*

Before stepping aside for faster runners to pass, I cannot resist a glimpse of our author: my friend, colleague, occasional aikido student and sometime running coach, Mike Spino, in the flesh: Most Saturdays or Sundays in

San Francisco, there is an open race sponsored by the Dolphin-South End Club, and what a joy it is to pour through the main street of Fisherman's Wharf or around Lake Merced or through Golden Gate Park or across the Golden Gate Bridge as part of a great mass of humanity, 300 to 800 strong, to the bemusement of tourists and the temporary discomfort of motorists. These aerobic pilgrims need not be embarrassed by lack of World Class speed; there's a gaily-colored ribbon for everyone who finishes. But up front at the start of the races are a hundred or so competitive runners who have come to vie for the first three places. Our Spino is among them, and every time I've been there he has managed to finish first or second.

My favorite of these events is called the Golden Gate Promenade Race, which starts at the San Francisco Marina and takes a route along the edge of the Bay to the base of the Golden Gate Bridge and back, a total distance of 3.7 miles. Outbound, you run into the teeth of an ocean breeze and there are sea gulls and sailboats and the spray of an occasional wave as the distant bridge gets closer and closer and finally looms over you like some monstrous science fiction movie set. Returning downwind, the splendid view seems to dissolve, and there's only the sound of your own breathing as counterpoint to the equally noisy panting and gasping all around you.

At such a race one recent Sunday morning, I was still some distance from the bridge when I encountered the front runners on their way back. And there, approaching me at a great speed, was our author, at least 200 yards in the lead. I want to assure you that I'm not given to visual hallucinations, but there was something about the way Spino was moving that caused a sudden lurch in my perceptions. It was as if, at the most exciting moment in a movie, the sound went off. He glided toward me silently in a sort of slow motion, with unbelievably long strides. Though the course was level, the earth seemed to tilt so that he appeared to be running downhill. His wet torso glistened through a black mesh T-shirt to give a silver-black cast to the space in which he moved, a space of about a hundred yards fore and aft which seemed to me absolutely inviolable. There was something uncanny about the liquid ease of his stride. Was he a giant wolf in human form? Why did his legs seem so long, so *stretched out?*

I've known Mike Spino for four years, since the beginning of the Esalen Sports Center, during which time he has lived an absolutely dedicated life. He has used his own body and being as a laboratory, not only pushing himself to the physical limit, but also practicing meditation and visualization and other mental-spiritual disciplines that he has joined to the physical. During that shimmering moment along the Golden Gate Promenade, I realized that his prodigious dedication was paying off. After the race, others who had been running near me confirmed my vision: Spino had been running magnificently, in a manner that could only be described as extradimensional. He himself was proof of his training methods.

As we passed, I heard myself shouting into the almost unbearable silence: "*Spino! Spino! It's the Transformation!*"

I have given you fair warning. Changing your way of running can change your life, sometimes in unexpected ways. Read on at your own risk.

—*George Leonard*

The Good Old Days

The running world has changed quite a bit since I began running 20 years ago. I first remember being timed as I ran to the store for groceries. In junior high school, we had to run across town for manual arts class. The first one there had 10 minutes to buy donuts in the local bakery. I always got there first.

At a recent road race I had a shot of nostalgia as I breathed in the smell of the "hot stuff" a few runners were rubbing into their legs. It reminded me of the 102nd Street Armory in New York City where races would be run on the eleven-laps-to-a-mile track from 9 A.M. to midnight on Saturdays during the winter months. The blacks would wear their hair in turbans, smell wonderful, and scream through rolled newspapers as someone would take off down the back straightaway. "Owooo," a high-pitched yell would resound through the auditorium. The Catholic schoolboys won most of the long-distance races—sleek, almost chiseled, looking incredibly clean. And there were the "track nuts," and Kenny was the supreme. At 5'4", a bit tubby and bleary-eyed, a former engineering major from City College, he now lived with his mother, and could be seen with four or five stopwatches around his neck. He would know the times of every kid who came to the track regularly.

A balding Irish bus mechanic, Peter McArdle, won all the road races. Oscar Moore from the Pioneer Club

1

would chase him through the Van Cortlandt Park hills. The great Canadian Bruce Kidd once beat them all, gaining ground up Cemetery Hill. Once I came over from Jersey and won a medal in a big race (all the veterans came straight from their night-shift jobs with running shoes stashed in brown paper bags). They didn't have the medals at the race, so three days later I took three buses and a train to pick up the medals. The office was closed.

The only place to get Adidas running shoes was at a warehouse on 76 Franklin Street. Our school didn't have a cross country team so I had to go over and beg for a pair without an official invoice. The owner told you what shoes to wear. If you didn't like it, no shoes.

Competition was the thing. At cross country meets in Van Cortlandt Park, 1,000 kids would run for the first turn a quarter mile down the green. As a Syracuse sophomore at the Pennsylvania relays, I ran three races in an hour and a half. Between the second and third I lay under the stadium, dazed and vomiting. That was 13 years ago.

Now thousands run or jog around tracks or through city streets. When did we stop having to climb fences to get to the track? What happened that people stopped giving you weird looks? and spitting on you when you ran? It used to be that the last thing anyone could understand was running. "Why should I run? No one is chasing me!" How many times have I felt real good while running only to have someone ask, "What place did you come in?"

Summer development meets: Waiting to take a bus to meet a car that would drive 300 miles to a track meet to which you were always late, usually got lost, and sometimes never had a chance to run. Running in snow-locked Syracuse, socks on hands, long johns, sometimes forced to run in the attic at Jack Scott's house because it was -10° outside with 5 feet of snow.

How did it all come to this—a running, jogging craze? How were the joys of running discovered by so many others? Is it physiological information? People afraid of getting old? Becoming less important to look substantial; more important to be healthy and vibrant? The California ethic? To do something really good for yourself with the least amount of time and effort? Jogging, running, fits the bill.

Now thousands run the streets in all kinds of costumes. Sometimes the fad scares me. All the platitudes and testimonials about something that was once so simple and esoteric. The good part is that it gets to be fun as your friends start to discover what you found out long ago. The new ethic takes the pressure off winning. It gets to be more and more fun to run. I am experiencing what those who meditate felt in the boom of the '60s, jazz artists felt in the '30s, the amazement that comes when what you have been doing naturally for many years becomes fascinating for thousands of others.

Why Run?...
I Want to Motivate You

Why exercise at all! What a bore, all the blokes going around and around the block or track worrying about falling dead if they don't exercise—obligation. But, what if you gave greater meaning to the act, had a deeper viewpoint for the activity?

When I first started writing this book I spent time thinking about the statement I wanted to make. It seemed evident that although we are a country which worships youth and results, we have millions of unhappy people. I have become convinced that the benefits of physical exercise, and the training effect that accompanies physical exertion is not automatically enough to allow a person a happy existence.

Happiness, and a sense of well-being, is more than a physiological outcome. Imagination coupled with fitness is exciting. Traditionally, physical fitness images in our culture have been shallow. As of late, these impressions are shifting. Today the runner is chic, fashionable, trendy.

Hundreds of books have been written about fitness. To write another book in this same vein, what a bore! It has all been done before, yesterday's business. What I seek to learn and what I attempt to teach is more a spirit change, an expanded sense of self. This can lead to a way of dealing with life from a vantage point of self-reliance and owning one's own personal power.

4

My teacher, Percy Cerutty, once said, "A man who is unfit is likely to be overconfident in the face of political and economic changes in the world." Yes, fitness can help you overcome fear, but I would hope our motivation can come from a higher level.

Fear. Primitive man often ran because he was fearful of the dark. It contained animals and perhaps evil spirits. When we understand the physiological benefits of running, will we run because we fear being left out, fear our bodies becoming decrepit early because we are not utilizing the secret? In his book, *The Ultimate Athlete*, George Leonard presents a wider reason. He says, "Searching for our Inner Athlete may lead us into sports and regular exercise and this to the health promised by physical fitness organizations—and that might be justification enough. But what I have in mind goes beyond fitness. It involves entering the realm of music, poetry, of the turning of the planets, of the understanding of death."

Eastern martial arts like Aikido, in which George is a black belt, teach activities with an orientation toward a larger vision. An expanded overview of the reason for a sport makes the activity more than physical. Can running, with new techniques and fresh reasons for the activity, become more than a physical discipline? This is a large part of our challenge.

What happens in our mechanized society is that we lose our spontaneity. We stop scheduling playtime; without release our emotional lives can become stilted. We have to make a choice to not accept half a life. As Cerutty says, "Don't wait for the hour of denouncement, the moment of truth, the pronouncement, or the good or bad prognosis, but feel emotion, arouse the intellect so that it, and the will, come into play." I know what being city-bound, desk-connected and family-oriented can mean. A bit of mindful physical action can be one key to a fuller lifestyle.

When you get into this program you aren't going to change overnight. But, step by step you will feel new layers of yourself unfold. The body will be the vehicle into this larger plan and scope. It will be the source of strength in inevitable periods of required fortitude and courage.

A New Vision

In the past, sport has meant winning and losing; historically, athletics have often been viewed as a form of war. There is a battle plan, a scheme of how to beat your opponent. In this context, when a holistic orientation which includes consciousness techniques is introduced into a training regimen, the question of many is "Will it allow me to run faster?"

Competitive athletes think in terms of winning. The person seeking better health concentrates on having and increasing energy necessary to compete in the commercial world. These over-stressed people realize they must do something. Obligation drives these people on. They can be found constantly checking their pulse, or obsessively counting laps.

Outside of these practicalities we have images of mind-body synthesis and harmony. We have been educated with stories of ancient Greece and Rome: A classical archetype of chariots and gladiators, drama and heroic poetry—an academy of mind, body, and spirit. These ideas are not easily transferred to our everyday lives. On the other hand belief in mystical events, psychic abilities or Eastern thought are too esoteric for the majority. Yet within these elements of potential influence lies an enormous interest in self-improvement, and physical as well as mental well-being. The people teaching this information at times work under the guise of gurus, healers, or shaman-types. The deep unconscious of most of us, at least as far as our bodies are concerned, carries the memories of our high-school gym teachers.

What becomes apparent is that a new view of sport, in this case running, is necessary. This calls for a shift in our overall concepts—paradigm changes. I believe it is a vast mistake to state the physiological benefits from exercise and to describe the peak experience resulting from sport without providing a framework from which to seek these places. To make fancy statements that leave people in limbo is unfair. Cerebral enthusiasm is not enough. It is my intention to spell out, point by point, basic physical conditioning shortcuts, consciousness techniques that get us in touch with basic awarenesses, and flexibility and exercises that induce calmness. In the instructional aspects I'll try to avoid titillating your imagination in favor of practical applications with sequential approaches that plan an individualized program, taking you from A to B to C.

I want to transform your daily jogging into a richer and more varied experience. When I wrote *Beyond Jogging*, I was mainly interested in formulating a theory based on the ideas of my teachers, Percy Cerutty and Mihaly Igloi, as they could be integrated into running for the average person. I wanted to show that running could be more fun than obligation. I explained ways of expanding the notion of cardiorespiratory conditioning. *Running Home* lays out methods and practices that will take you through six weeks that will improve your health while integrating awareness and consciousness techniques, and suppleness and flexibility exercises with running.

As a competitive runner in my early twenties I had some remarkable experiences that I can only describe as "spiritual situations." No one was available to counsel me on what was transpiring. On one particular run I had the sensation of running like a skeleton through a wind tunnel, of losing my identity during a fast six-mile run. These experiences were veiled. My interest was in fast timings, and improving my position in the pecking order with racing rivals. What I didn't realize was that I had this "floaty feeling" during the most successful athletic endeavors, and that achievement was an end product of integrated personality and self-realization. I didn't put together cause and effect.

If you follow the discipline presented in *Running Home* you will improve your physical performance. If you take the exercises as secret weapons to enable you to win, you will suffer frustration. For instance, I am running a very hard race. There are 7,000 people in this 7.8-mile race, the annual Bay-to-Breakers in San Francisco. Before the race I sat in a room where 1,500 people were roaming about, going to the toilet, joking and jousting to ward off tension. Instead of joining in the excitement I sat quietly, closing my eyes. My legs were shaking with anxiety. After a few minutes of sitting quietly I had the sensation of taking in all the excess energy being released in the room. I walked to the starting line where thousands of people swarmed. I saw scared people, athletes going to war, funsters dressed in tuxedo-type running outfits. I found a place near the side and got into my own awareness. I want to know who I am, standing on the street with 7,000 other people preparing to run 7.8 miles. I want to know because my goal is self-understanding. Knowing makes life more meaningful for me. It can give me reassurance and confidence.

If I know who I am at the start of a meaningless (in a sense), 7,000-person race, perhaps I might have the courage to ask who I am in more dire situations—death, love—situations needing all my courage. It doesn't necessarily have to be that heavy, but it might be. In a way I am as alone and self-contained as if I was at home sitting during morning meditation.

The start of the race had been a mob scene. Thousands in a charge. Then it separates out and you are running in a small group, then with one other person. Your breathing becomes labored. You are thinking about just making it to the finish line. Then you remember a story a friend told you about surrendering. It was a tale about surviving torture—a Buddhist story. The idea doesn't all hold together because you are running at a near five-minute mile pace, and there is an unpleasant nausea in your stomach. The pain begins to set in; I am at the five-mile mark.

The story line again. The Buddhist taught that if you could just stay in the moment without present, past or future you could live through almost anything. But the realization must be authentic, not feigned. The reason for staying in the moment is to experience life, not beat the torturer. If this running is my way of being in the world, then at this moment I am what I intended to be. The pain is me. I am properly doing my unique form of living. It is my destiny.

If I can surrender to the situation and, in surrendering, give up the result and live only to fully know the uneasiness, the run becomes spiritual. I close my eyes for an instant without falling, without loss of balance, as I go inside to observe my movements I notice I am not going "that fast," and the uneasiness becomes more familiar. It is a deep part of all that I am.

Soon the finish line looms around a corner. I pour into the run. Now, with abandon I gallop towards a finish, a temporary ending. In those few seconds I am totally happy. Then it is over, joy and ennui. I grasp my opponent in a hug. I touch his hand, he understands and then pulls back into himself. Soon I am only one in a mass of people, it is a festival of satisfaction, frustration, and release from the obligation of finishing under your own best effort. The event is easily forgotten, but the development of a style of viewing the run has made it more important.

How to be a Runner
Rather than a Jogger

If you are one who has jogged around your block for many days without showing much improvement and are beginning to feel bored, I would like to suggest a new way of going about the activity. Time yourself over a mile, or see how far you can run in six minutes. The reason I am suggesting a mile or a six-minute effort is that it combines the perfect balance of breathing and changes in style of movement that, when properly utilized in a comprehensive program, will result in optimum physical fitness.

The primary point is that in order for your physical conditioning to improve substantially you must vary your metabolic system (breathing), and your way of moving or running. Let me give an example of the way your body breathes. Suppose you establish two points one hundred yards apart and plan to cover the distance between these points in a number of ways. If you first run 100 yards at 50 percent effort and walk back to the starting position, by the time you reach the starting position your breathing will be totally recovered. If you run the 100 yards a second time at 50 percent, and jog back to the starting line you may be slightly out of breath. If you again run the 100 yards in 50 percent effort; rest just a few seconds and immediately head back to the starting position at 50 percent effort, at the half way point you will begin running out of breath.

Your body in this third effort has changed its way of

11

breathing, and its style of running. It has gone into the changes that must happen when you are running a mile near maximum effort. If these shifts aren't practiced, as when you jog at a constant tempo, the rate of physical improvement is lessened. Your body cannot do what it hasn't practiced.

If John Walker, the world-record holder in the mile (3:49.4), were to run a mile each day for his practice he would probably be able to run the mile no faster than a 4:15. The knowledge that has gone into his training is derived from a historical evolution of the means of achieving peak physical functioning. I want to give you this information, and blend it with the other uses of running or jogging that are making it America's fastest growing recreation.

Let's look, then, at the way the body operates while running. In all of running there are only three ways in which the body can work. These are aerobically, anaerobically, and for speed. The degree of exercise, in these terms, is measured by the rate of oxygen consumption and the lactic acid concentration in the blood. We use the term *aerobic* and *anaerobic* to refer to the presence or absence of oxygen in the muscle cells and other cells of the body. There are a number of good explanations of this process which goes from relatively unstrenuous running to full effort. E. C. Frederick, a physiologist from Flagstaff, Arizona says, "If we are performing an exercise so strenuous that the need for the oxygen in the cells exceeds the capability of our bodies to take up and transport oxygen to these tissues, then we are exercising in an anaerobic state. If the demand for oxygen doesn't exceed the supply, then the exercise is aerobic. Seldom is an exercise either/or." Laurence E. Morehouse, the man who authored the book *Total Fitness*, describes the process as follows: "If a person engages in mild exercise there is no oxygen deficit during exercise (aerobic), that is, a steady state exists, and there is no excess oxygen consumption during recovery. If the exercise is somewhat more strenuous (anaerobic), the oxygen consumption during recovery is above the resting level, indicating an oxygen deficit during the exercise."

In reality, while running we usually go between aerobic and anaerobic states. Certain distances have inherent ratios of aerobic to anaerobic metabolic rates. These include a marathon (26 plus miles) which is 95 percent aerobic, and 5 percent anaerobic, a 100-yard dash which is 5 percent aerobic and 95 percent anaerobic, and the mile which is an even 50 percent aerobic/50 percent anaerobic. David Costell, a leading physiologist at Ball State University, describes the aerobic/anaerobic split as follows: "Aerobic exercise means that the individual can sustain prolonged exercise because his oxygen consumption during exercise is sufficient to meet the demands of active muscles. However, if one is not able to meet the oxygen demands of exercise via his oxygen uptake, he must draw upon the anaerobic reserves of the body."

In addition to aerobic and anaerobic exercise is sprinting. We define sprinting as running more than 70 percent of your maximum effort. If an exercise is very strenuous, oxygen consumption during recovery is large (it takes time to get back to normal breathing), *and* the blood lactic acid concentration is elevated. After a time the rate of oxygen consumption and the blood lactic acid concentration gradually returns to normal. Metabolically sprinting is mostly anaerobic. If a run is less than 15 seconds, lactic acid, the substance that poisons the body during intensive running, does not accumulate. The enemy is lactic acid. Once it enters the muscles it takes a long period for the muscles to recuperate. Rodolfo Margaria is the leading researcher in the fatigue factor of lactic acid. He has found a way to "cheat" the fatigue system. Margaria says the lactic acid mechanism is sluggish. It takes about 15 seconds to snap into action during an all-out run. But once activated it drives the runner to exhaustion within the next 15–20 seconds.

"Because there is always a certain period of delay in the onset of lactic acid production even in highly strenuous exercise," Margaria notes, "one can avoid this production by limiting the activity period to a short enough time." I have planned workouts with runs less than 15 seconds in duration in which we run at near maximum speed, but at a short enough distance so that the fatigue factor of lactic acid does not accumulate. This will aid greatly in our preparation for the mile run.

By using these facts you can move from being a jogger into a runner who has conditioned the body to the experiences it must master if it is to run smoothly, efficiently, and pleasurably. In other words, when someone only jogs or sprints they do not prepare their body for the various levels of metabolic function and styles of movement that come into play when a person engages in strenuous activity. The body can only accomplish what it has practiced and experienced.

When a person only uses one rhythm, as in jogging, they usually improve to a certain level and then find it difficult to even keep at the level they have attained. This is because the individual has ceased working to extend his potential. To improve after the initial aerobic build-up takes variety; what a person takes to be boredom may in actuality be physiological. The uses of varied tempos and gaits of running, especially when they are combined with auxiliary running styles and awareness techniques, make it an easier discipline. At a time of demanding priorities, shortcuts are desirable, if not absolutely necessary. I believe this approach also enhances spontaneity and self-reliance, and makes it possible to enjoy a fitness program.

In developing these ideas, let's blend the information into a practical way of looking at the concept of jogging. First, jogging is primarily defined according to the tempo. That is, a person who is running a 7:30-mile pace or slower is said to be jogging. We add to this metabolic definition particular styles of movement: For instance, one can run at a *shuffle* (landing on the heels with awareness below the knee), or at *fresh swing* tempo (lifting the knee, stepping out in a cyclical motion while being aware of the natural foot plant on the outside of the foot).

If you jog at one pace, or use a derivative utilizing the shuffle and fresh swing you can expect to produce the training effect of aerobic fitness discovered by Dr. Kenneth Cooper, author of *Aerobics*, after testing more than a million beginning runners.

These effects include:

- Lungs which take in and distribute oxygen more efficiently.

- Bigger and more blood vessels capable of carrying larger amounts of blood.

- Increased volume of blood with a greater total oxygen-carrying capacity.

- Healthier body tissue as a result of oxygen abundance.

- Strong, healthy heart which is "slow at rest," yet capable of accelerating to much higher work loads without undue fatigue or strain.

- Smoother digestion of food and elimination of wastes.

- Mental benefits including reduction in anxiety and irritability, improved ability to relax and sleep.

Isn't this enough? What more can you expect! I say it is not enough. We know more about how the body functions, and we are learning more all the time about how to blend our consciousness with our running. By integrating consciousness with running, our overall fitness can go beyond the training effect in the same amount of time with more physical and psychological pleasure. The training effect is a measurement produced by medical research. However, the mind/body synthesis is better handled by master teachers and their adherents.

My plan for improving your mile run or the distance you can cover in 6 minutes is based on combinations of ways of training for running. I have chosen these two methods for our assessment because they produce the perfect balance between aerobic and anaerobic metabolism, and could potentially account for a tremendous upswing in fitness of all who would improve their ability to cover the mile.

Each of the methods of running has a specific purpose. The workouts are laid out over a 6-week period in a particular order so that your body can adapt to the training, and reach various levels and plateaus most efficiently. The terms most used in the context of the workout will be *gait* and *tempo*. *Tempo* is the amount of effort required during a particular run. *Gait* is the specific style of movement used to accomplish the particular segment.

Fartlek running was first developed in Scandinavia in the 1940s by runners Gunder Hagg and Arne Anderson under the coaching of Gosta Holmer. Fartlek, which means "speed play" in Swedish, has been said to resemble the play of children. Added to jogging it would mean speeding up or increasing the tempo either spontaneously, or for a prescribed distance or time. Some practices include using telephone poles as markers (they are 100 yards apart), and running with a partner, each sharing the lead and determining the distance to be run. Fartlek training was responsible for bringing the mile record down from 4:08 to 4:01.

When we add fartlek running to *long slow distance* training, we enable our bodies to spontaneously shift between aerobic and anaerobic metabolism. But, I find it necessary to be a bit more precise than leaving these changes to personal discretion. Authoritative supports bring faster results, like a new tree being staked to grow straight and tall. Therefore, I include *interval* running.

The main difference between fartlek running and interval training is that fartlek is done on a forest path or open road with an open-ended plan, while an interval workout usually takes place on a track or grass section inside or around a running track.

This type of training was formalized in the 1930s by two German doctors, Woldermar Gerschler, a physiologist-coach, and Hans Reindell, a cardiologist. In the form of interval running we will incorporate the techniques of Mihaly Igloi, the Hungarian immigrant who brought American distance running up to world class in the late 1950s and 1960s. Interval training is a system of repeated efforts in which a measured distance is run with a measured recovery period of low activity. One goal of interval training is to increase general endurance by enlarging the heart. As fartlek is a free-form run, intervals are preplanned and usually done for a specific purpose. A group of intervals run for a specific purpose, such as running 100 yards at a fast speed to increase tempo ability, is called a set. The beauty of interval running is the specificity of aerobic and anaerobic ratios possible by shifting the distance, tempo, and recovery period.

For instance, if we took six distances, used fresh swing, shuffle, and other tempos in a formula which had four varied rest periods, we could utilize specific physiological states precisely to the level of effort we want to create. This precision enables you to get in shape faster.

Gerschler and Reindell discovered that, "Running effort in interval training should send the heart beat to around 180 beats per minute. When this happens the heart should be allowed 90 seconds to return to 120–125 beats per minute. If it takes longer the effort demanded has either been too violent or too long." The physiologist Costill adds, "When the heart rate reaches 180 beats per minute it no longer benefits the individual to continue the exercise, as the heart can neither fill nor empty completely."

I have taken care to formalize the workouts in the six-week program so that the body is not forced beyond 180 beats per minute. In this program, each interval has the same amount of rest period. For instance, if you run 100 yards at fresh swing tempo, you will walk or shuffle 100 yards as the recovery. The only exception is a technique called the shake-up which enables you to complete a warm-up. In the shake-up there is no interval rest period.

Your level of effort can be measured by taking your pulse rate. Don't overstrain, you achieve more by striving against your physiological limits. A primary goal is to reach a place where you are running powerfully, able to call on your reserves to accelerate when you wish.

Added to the long, slow running of the shuffle and fresh swing, and the fartlek and interval training, will be sprinting (speed work), and resistance running. Sprinting goes beyond the balanced aerobic/anaerobic ratio. If you are running over 80 percent of your maximum effort for a period of more than 15 seconds lactic acid will accumulate in the body. Speed work is an extremely powerful tool. M. M. Yakovlov, a Russian physiologist, reports, "Training by short, fast exercises of maximal and submaximal intensity led to varied adoption by increasing the potential range of both aerobic and anaerobic provisions of energy for work." And D. B. Dill, writing in *Sports Medicine and Physical Fitness*, adds, "Sprinting allows increased capacity for supplying oxygen and at the same time commits higher levels of energy exchange *before* the lactic acid debts begin to accumulate." Sprinting is flowing or a better term, pouring, the practice of moving your legs quickly, and running with small supplies of oxygen.

Lee Evans still holds the world record in the 400 meters (43.86 set in 1968 Olympics). During his last year with the International Track Association he worked with the Esalen Sport Center. We ran a lot of miles together that particular summer, as Lee wanted to make the transition from the sprints to the middle distances. One day when we were out training Lee asked me to run as fast as I could in any direction I wanted. I gathered up my limited resources and barrelled across the field as quickly as I could. Before I knew it a flash went by me. It was a body that moved like a perfectly balanced machine and a little boy at the same time. That was Lee Evans sprinting.

But Lee wasn't always that smooth, and I remember him holding on at the finish of extremely close races. Bud Winters, his coach at San Jose State, taught the sprinters a process to enable the body to keep its forward momentum by consciously eliminating the symptoms of fighting off lactic acid—raising the arms, clenching teeth, swaying shoulders, etc. In order to keep knees high with a full reach of the legs, he taught sprinters to reach out as though shaking hands and to let air pull the elbow back into a vacuum, and visualize running a foot above the head while chanting.

Percy Cerutty did most of the pioneering work in strength and resistance conditioning. He found that fitness could be greatly improved by strengthening the muscles directly by the use of hills, sand dunes, barbells or special techniques such as the *power run* (a way of simulating resistance running by placing the weight of the body against itself). The running we do up dunes, hills, stairs, or in the power run is designed so that the muscles are put against stress, somewhat like weight lifting for the legs. In the right dosage this kind of running can give additional power that running on flat surfaces cannot accomplish. In most training it is beneficial to run on flat surfaces, because when the foot lands on a flat surface the leg muscles are able to go through their entire sequence of tensing and relaxing. This promotes fitness. But in resistance conditioning it is best to locate a place distinct from your regular running area to specifically practice musculoskeletal power.

There are a number of ways to use resistance techniques. The first is the gradual hill. Find an uphill grade at a moderate angle that takes about a minute and a half to run. It can be either dirt or cement. Divide the distance into three segments. Run either of the segments but only at 50 percent effort. Don't mince your stride and keep the arms relatively low. Other forms of resistance running can be performed on sand dunes and city steps. The best surfaces are grass or sand. Begin at only 15 or 20 yards.

Driving to a picturesque dune occasionally can be a form of spiritual pilgrimage. One of my favorite places is a sand hill on the beach at Santa Cruz near St. Francis Camp. I will run sets of six to ten dunes, and then sit quietly in meditation. I have an urge at these times to destroy myself, to run the dune until I reach exhaustion. A friend's interpretation of these impulses is that by destroying myself, by disintegrating, I could come together at a higher level of being. After one such incident I lamented the separation of mind and body: the labyrinthine and extremely intricate passageway of the mind and its unconscious; the purity but vulnerability of the physical; the fine web and connection in between.

At the proper time, a resistance workout can add dynamite to your training ritual. It can get you out of a rut like nothing else. Power running is a great substitute for resistance conditioning. The object of this exercise is not linear movement, but a striving, lifting up motion that builds overall muscle and spirit power. Moving, reaching up at the sky, the tension of self against self, creates power.

Through the judicious use of large doses of resistance work one of Cerutty's pupils, Herb Elliott, ran the mile under 3:55 for the first time in 1958.

The *shuffle* derives from information I received from Bill Emmerton, the ultra-long-distance runner. Bill has accomplished such feats as a run across Death Valley, and another from Houston to Cape Kennedy to inaugurate the first moon launching (58 miles a day for 28 days). When I asked Bill how he did it he said, "They say I run, but actually I go at 12-13-minute mile pace. I shuffle." The shuffle then is for warming up or moving slowly over long distances. The foot plant is far back on the heel. You push out from the knees with awareness focused low on the legs. The arm action that aids in shuffling is to carry one arm across the body in front of the belly, and a counter movement directed slightly forward with the opposite arm. This should only be done at less than 20 percent of your potential effort. Some people may develop problems with their calves or shins because they don't shift into faster gaits when traveling over 20 percent effort.

If you want to increase your tempo from a shuffle you should run at a gait called *fresh swing* tempo. Fresh swing is done with 20 to 40 percent of your maximum effort—at first these degrees won't mean much, but after running 10 or so intervals you can estimate fairly accurately the degree of effort of a particular run. As you go faster the body automatically lifts the knee; when you lift the knee and step out, you naturally step on the outside of the foot and slightly up from the heel. This doesn't require special practice, it should happen naturally. You can aid by rolling forward off the outside of the foot, so that instead of lifting the foot at each step you roll into the next step. If you want to go faster than a shuffle, increase the tempo by lifting the knee slightly, step out and roll from the outside of the foot inward.

Good swing tempo is the same motion but with an intensity of 40 to 80 percent effort—beyond 80 percent effort you are sprinting.

The *shake-up* is used for completing a warm-up or at the end of a workout. It is the final preparation of the body for full action. The shake-up is opposed to sprinting hard a few times before you are prepared to do serious training. In the shake-up, let all the muscles hang on your skeleton as if you were a rag doll while moving up and down. Alternate from the toes to the back of the foot, sometimes in regular rhythm, other times in choppy short steps. It is possible for people to go into difficult training directly from shake-ups, while others will still experience some stiffness after sprinting warm-up intervals.

Combining the different methods of running with these basic tempos will bring fast conditioning. You will notice when you begin to run distances like a 660 or three-quarters of a mile that your breathing and style of movement seems more appropriate and your effort will seem more fluid. Your training will have been specific for the result in your final assessment—a mile run or six-minute run—and you will feel comfortable in greater physical efforts.

What you will be doing is a combination of these methods in a rounded format that will lead to a new level of fitness. The majority of fitness programs explain the wonders of exercise, but fail to present a progression that will produce results. How do you get from A to B? I have given you a detailed description, complete with time assessments, calculating the plateaus of conditioning that you will reach during the six-week program. For the participant who finds it difficult to keep to a detailed schedule there is a short-term version. For the person who wants only to maintain health there are auxiliary forms.

Using a varied system of training you can get in shape much quicker than with simple jogging. By running long distances slowly, doing precise intervals, sprinting occasionally, and running spontaneously on open roads and up hills, you will quickly come to optimum physical condition. Through my experience I have collected techniques that master coaches teach to give their students that extra edge. Most of the practices are taken from the work of Igloi and Cerutty, and the innerspace techniques we have developed at the Esalen Sports Center.

One of the easiest ways to increase ability is through breathing. Many people ask if they should breathe through the nose or through the mouth. In natural running you just let the air come in any way it can, usually through both the nose and mouth. The important thing in regular gaits is not the way the air is taken in but the relaxation of the face and neck. A tongue that flaps loose in the mouth is a sign of running without tension. To increase your endurance in running, the object is to utilize all of your lung capacity—full lung aeration.

One tool you can use to propel yourself forward is called *tidal breathing*. To begin, take a breath, and blow the air out as if you were blowing out a candle. You will notice after all the breath is out the lungs immediately suck air back in. The easiest way to get fresh air into your lungs is to blow out the air that is already inside them. You can use your arms to help.

First, practice while you are standing in place. As you breathe in, let your hands, palms upward, rise next to the body. Imagine your upper body to be an elevator, and as

you raise your arms, let the air flow inward. At the top of the breath, hold it for a split second to build up velocity—store the energy until the time to release. As the breath comes out, push down the arms, palms facing the ground and let your body be propelled forward.

Begin running at a shuffle, and when you make the transition into the fresh swing do so by using tidal breathing to push yourself forward. When I teach this technique near the ocean I have students watch the waves break out of the corner of their eye, measuring their exhale with the cresting of the wave. This helps to vary each breath. It is variability and spontaneity of breathing

that allows you to increase your endurance.

A shortcut version of tidal breathing is *shoulder breathing*. While you are running along, lift your shoulders as you take in air. On the exhale, let yourself be propelled forward. A helpful visualization is to picture yourself 20 yards in front of your current position. When you breathe out, catch up to the place you visualized yourself being, 20 yards ahead.

In our usual swing tempo the foot plant is near the back of the foot, rolling inward from the outside. This is the natural foot plant when you are running without conscious effort. But, if you can change the foot plant to behind the toes, even for 20 yards, the muscles used throughout the body change. This changing of the foot plant can be accompanied by a shifting of the use of the arms from "puller" to a "rhythm-maker." Instead of the arms being held at the sides, they are held in front almost as though you were playing drums, but with both hands together. This technique is called *good speed*. It is used when accelerating into faster tempos, or when beginning to falter, or for a quick acceleration. Usually, good speed is done at 50 percent effort.

The best way to learn to run at good speed is to first practice what it feels like to run "behind the toes." This can be done by experimenting with this tempo for five or ten yards a few times. Walk along and then stay behind your toes with the foot plant for a few yards. Then run an interval, breaking the distance into thirds: Run the first third at shuffle; the next at good speed, changing the foot plant to behind the toes and using the arms as a balancer rather than puller; and then make the transition to swing tempo. You will find this technique very helpful for resting the legs, and for getting out of a rut when you are stuck in a particular tempo.

Percy Cerutty invented the *surge* as a technique to use in battling near the completion of a race. It is a way of gathering your energy for the final spurt toward the tape. In our practice we will use the surge mainly as a focusing tool to drive forward more easily, thereby raising pulse beat and breathing apparatus to a higher level of work.

In a competitive situation the surge works something like this: Focus on someone in front of you. Visualize throwing a rope out and hooking your opponent around the neck. Pull the rope toward you as though you were reeling a fish in on a line. As you begin to approach your opponent, open your hands, slightly crouch, and stretch your fingers out, then cup them, pinch your fingers and make a "ping" sound in your throat and into your opponent's ear. The person will tighten for a split second as you charge forward. After going by, shake your head slightly to further disorient your opponent. It is very difficult for someone to recover and make a quick comeback if you do it right.

Also use the surge to increase your speed during an interval. Let yourself begin with a fresh swing, and about three-fourths into an interval, open the hands, stretch them, cup the hands, press the thumb and first finger together, make a "ping" sound in the throat and with a sound like that in a karate chop let yourself go forward. Don't worry about your feet, just let yourself be thrown forward and allow the momentum to carry you to the end of your chosen run. The touch between the thumb and first finger can be thought of as pressing on the accelerator of a car.

Sprint form is a way to practice maintaining your body at the crucial times when lactic acid is hitting the body while you are trying to go at the fastest tempo possible. When you are tiring, the physics of your forward motion is affected.

This can be practiced at the seashore, the track, or a flat grass field. Use an interval of about 40 to 60 yards, four times. The first time, run the distance to see how much you can lift your knees. On the second interval extend this practice to see how far you can reach out; you will be running with high knees and a full leg reach. On the third interval, add a visualization: picture yourself reaching out to shake hands with someone, and then visualize a force of air pulling your elbow back alternately, so that you will now be running with high knees, a full leg reach, and reaching out to shake hands with someone and letting a force of air pull your arm back. The fourth interval includes an embellishment on the third: visualize yourself running a foot above your head, chant through your teeth, and run with high knees and a full leg reach, visualizing yourself reaching outward and letting a force of air pull your elbow back.

The use of Percy Cerutty's techniques—the trot, canter, and gallop—have caused me much reflection. This form of naturalistic running was to be his final synthesis—five movements leading to the ultimate gait, the gallop. Percy had it worked out that the gallop would enable modern people to run as do animals and people in primitive states, in unison with nature—undulating and asymmetrical. His idea was to experience labored breathing and then flow with it; to be driving out on the outbreath, and floating on the intake; in the drive outward to get a bit of a jump, a bounce to make the odd asymmetrical step longer with the same amount of effort needed in a regular stride. Percy had a mathematician at his training camp at Portsea, Australia, figure out that running at a gallop, a 3:54 mile would translate into a 3:47 mile.

It was difficult for me to fully integrate these "naturalistic" techniques into my teachings because few competitive runners seemed to gallop (newsreels of Herb Elliott running didn't seem to show any significant difference between his style and the style of other runners). But I had learned to gallop, and at times would demonstrate the gaits as Percy described them. My fear was that people would get into trying these movements, and it would hamper their progress in attaining overall physical fitness. As my own practice developed I was able to canter occasionally to counteract the tension that built up in hard running, or as a style to run relaxed and fluid.

But sometimes it didn't work for me, and when I taught it people occasionally looked ridiculous. I questioned the validity of Percy's teachings. Had he become senile in his old age?

I came at first to a compromise. I would show the full form—stretch up, amble, trot, canter, gallop—to young children whose patterns of movement had not yet been developed. I would teach it to overweight and endomorphic people—I figured anything they did was a benefit. For a while I taught the gallop only on special occasions; I curtailed the teachings in my regular workshops.

At the end of every workshop someone would ask about the canter and gallop, and I would become evasive. They had read about asymmetrical, naturalistic running in *Beyond Jogging*, and wanted to know what it looked like, and what it could accomplish. After all, they said, "We are running for fun, not to win races."

I was giving a workshop at Oasis Center in Chicago. We were running up a local city street. I was about to end the session when someone asked about the gallop and I began to be evasive in giving my arguments. They said, "Look, we aren't competitive runners. We have the room to experiment. We don't have to run a race on Saturday." We went through the process and had a ball, cantering up the street. Since then it has been part of my repertoire.

Naturalistic Running

There is a five-part progression into the gallop. The process begins with the *stretch-up*. In the stretch-up exhale all the air out of your lungs while you stretch the entire body just as a cat does before taking off on a run— throw both arms overhead, exhale, and make a sighing sound. As the arms come down from the highest reach, let air flow back into the lungs, but instead of letting the arms return to a forward position, bring them up the sides of the body, and exhale by throwing the arms straight forward out in front. While doing this *amble* you should have begun to move forward, but not very much. Move from this amble into the trot, the third part of the progression. The breath is again drawn in, and the arms dropped, palms down in front of the body. Rather than a thrust downward, as in tidal breathing in which you wish to pick up velocity, in the trot let the drop of the arms be like the dropping of tension.

In all of the preceding techniques, there was no concern with footfall, and the stride was evenly taken. In the *canter* and *gallop* this is changed. Before going to the canter, though, practice a few times: stretch up, amble, trot . . .

For the *canter* choose a lead arm and a follow arm. The motion is crawl-like, and you will be running in a skipping motion. Reach with the lead arm (my lead arm is my left and the right my follow; this means the thrust will be off

my right foot), breathe out and you will propel yourself forward.

Arms are first carried along the sides as in fresh or good swing. As the energy begins to build, the palm comes up and then turns and reaches out. The theory is that one can float on the inhale and only work when the maximum distance can be accomplished with the appropriate style. The *gallop* is just an extension of the canter with a further reaching out. Do the canter and gallop for fun, for a heightened sense of the way your body can move. Don't worry if you can't run as fast cantering as just running. You may express something deep in your primitive unconscious. That is as important as running fast over a given distance.

The Six-Week Schedule

The combination of workouts in the six-week schedule are a mixture of the various elements of the running program. They are put together in a form that is usable for people who range in ability to run the mile from 4:30 to 15 minutes. The schedule is based on five workouts a week because that has been shown to be the most efficient use of the time most people are willing to allot to personal fitness. Each ten days there will be a workout provided that allows one to catch up if a day is missed, then continue with the planned workouts. Mental practices should be done, whenever possible, in conjunction with the actual running and especially during the easy gaits. Those mental practices that require complex visual imagining need separate space.

The uniqueness of this six-week "recipe" is that it can be applied to people of all levels of health or fitness. If you take a mile test and repeat this mile six weeks later, you should have an improvement, one that may be significant. This routine is planned to take you through the necessary rhythm and patterns toward improved physical condition, giving thought to the fact the body needs time to develop muscle tone, that physical improvement comes in stages and plateaus, and that rest is as important as activity, sometimes more so. For instance, intervals with a long rest period done at fresh gaits are a necessity for building endurance if you have done no physical exercise

34

for a number of years. On the other hand, if you were to have the rest period between these intervals shortened to perhaps a few seconds you would be running on a reserve, breathing hard, and using a metabolic function incompatible with your present state of health. It would be like taking money out of your bank account when you have little capital. You are not prepared for the investment.

High-level anaerobic exercises, like sprinting, don't build the aerobic power necessary for building our initial foundation for fitness. We focus on fresh gaits that give a slight amount of winding. This breezy feeling is helping improve your condition, and seems easier than the drudgery of jogging. When anything is done within a natural rhythm it flows. This flow causes pleasurable feelings, kinesthetic pleasures. In short, the proper workout and the correct sequence of conditioning based on principles of physical improvement necessitate what might seem like an authoritarian approach.

Some may complain that the flow of their lives makes it impossible to follow such a strict course of training, that this closely monitored program takes away from the freedom they previously enjoyed while running and threatens their sense of identity. I sympathize and am very familiar with all that goes on around the issue of scheduling. There was a time when a coach who gave a specific schedule was suspect—how could he know how each athlete would feel every day? Many teachers, including my mentor Percy Wells Cerutty, would not give exact schedules. But Percy had an ashram setting in a seaport 60 miles outside of Melbourne, Australia. If I had everyone who reads this book at Portsea we would meet only occasionally and the setting would inspire an innately spiritual way of mind and body. But today, it seems most practical to plan 30 minutes five times a week for workouts.

This tightly structured six-week program becomes necessary because people need a guideline in their physical conditioning to take maximum advantage of the limited time available. I am saddened by the hordes that visit a track stadium, run a few laps the same way in the same pace for months and end up improving their condition very little. The diversity of the workout I present will loosen the spirit, and the sense of play and change will put you into the rhythm of life, constantly changing.

If you go through the six weeks wholeheartedly, not arguing the logic of the workouts, staying with your own physical process (don't finish something that is too much of a strain), I believe you will find that the six weeks will go quickly and the variety will make it all the more pleasurable. You will benefit if even on those bad days when it just doesn't feel good, you will run at least 50 percent of the workout, or by substituting your long, slow distance training—don't worry about pushing yourself.

How to Set Up Your Course

You will want to gain as many benefits from the program as quickly as possible. In order to do so, it is necessary to seek out the correct environment. It may even be necessary to drive a few minutes to a location at which specific kinds of workouts can be done. Don't let a short ride keep you from doing the proper training. Usually the best place is a track with a football field in the middle, and adjacent fields. Begin by laying out the distances you want to utilize. If you are working on a standard 440-yard track, the inside grass can be calibrated into a 330, a horseshoe that begins and ends into the turns, 220 yards measured from the beginning of a turn to reduce the amount of turning, and 150 yards off the turn or on a long straightaway. A 100-yard sprint can be done on the inside grass of the football field. The 330, 220 and 150 can be done on the inside grass or the actual track surface. The track surface is better suited for the more intense tempos. Use the largest circumference of the field for warm-up shuffling.

Next, measure out near your house a road to use for fartlek and LSD (long, slow distance) conditioning. This road should be fairly flat. It is nice if the side of the road has a dirt surface strip so that you are free to run on it or the road. Fartlek, spontaneous interval running, is directed toward free-flowing bursts, and the measurements can be done in either time or distance. The

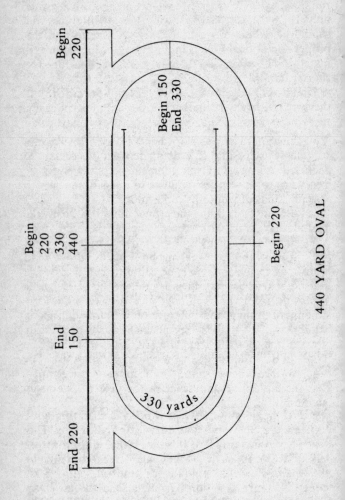

440 YARD OVAL

resistance efforts can be done separately from the other running. As these muscle resistance intervals constitute only 10 percent of the first month's conditioning you should be willing to travel a short distance to find the proper conditions. Find a long sloping surface approximately a 30° angle, and (ideally) a sand hill or dune for shorter bursts.

The workouts over the six weeks will be varied, but they will follow a particular pattern and be of a type easily recognized. The types of workouts, and their particular sequence have been chosen after much scrutiny, and the experience of applying similar workouts to thousands of people in the last five years I have been teaching and developing this method.

The techniques and approaches contained in the six-week program are the result of my study with two of the most successful track coaches in the history of running. The terminology is made up from the ideas of Mihaly Igloi of Hungary and Percy Wells Cerutty of Australia. Of the two, Cerutty was the more spirited. His training camp was an athletic "religious" retreat. But Percy's true ambition was to help humanity through teaching physical fitness, and he professed a mysticism that was not easily defined in the athletic terms of his day—so they called him an iconoclast. My consideration for using his approaches is based on their suitability for integration with awareness methods and ways of teaching fostered by the human potential movement.

Your running over the six weeks will be based on the ratio of 65 percent endurance, 25 percent speed or tempo and 10 percent resistance running. All along the way there will be "time trials" or assessments of your improvement. The last week will be spent on developing speed, creaming off the month's physical build-up.

The gaits in endurance running are shuffle, fresh swing, and shake-up. The speed or tempo running is good speed, good swing, surge, tidal breathing, trot, canter.

Power or resistance running is done up different grades of hills.

The training chart that appears in this book allows each member of the group or family to be working at the same field, in a similar, but individually tailored workout. Ideally, part of each workout can be done together by the entire group. In any event, the workout period should be planned to accommodate all family members.

A typical week in the first part of the running program will include an interval workout, fartlek training, LSD, shuffle/fresh swing, and a combination of workouts that includes speed and resistance running. For the very young or endomorphic, specialized techniques will be offered. A pattern that has one workout difficult and the next easy will be applied. Each division will have a workout specially prepared if a day is missed. This will only be on the ratio of one day to fourteen. If two or three days are missed you can turn the calendar back and work retroactively. Beyond this you must be in the 'catch as you can' category. Workouts can be picked out with some results but no series of rationales for training will be in operation.

Innerspace work will be done as part of actual running as well as in separate sessions. Relaxation and mental rehearsal techniques will precede some training efforts. Practices that include visualizations, breathing, techniques, and altered state approaches to fitness can be done with the easy gaits. In relation to internal work, a diary should be kept to record experiences, physical progress and random thoughts.

Interval running workouts should be done on an open grass field. The inside of a track or adjacent areas will be okay. If possible, map out a loop around the entire outside of the field. Use this space for warming-up and for rests between sets of intervals. If possible, do shuffle and warm-up exercises together as a group. This will be followed by shake-ups, and in some cases the first few intervals can be run together as a group. Each set of interval workouts has its own rationale, and the 25 percent speed or tempos aspect of your running will be covered in these workouts. In the beginning weeks, all running intervals will be followed by a rest period of the same duration. These intervals at first should be done at one steady pace. In the later weeks, build-ups in which the first half of an interval is slower than the second half can be instituted (these are called *negative intervals*).

One thing to remember while interval training is to "settle in" before each run. If you begin an interval off balance, you probably will carry this form throughout. One tremendous grace in the intervals is that you will be on the track with other people, but not have to get into their "treadmill" mentality. I assure you that 90 percent of the people at the track will be running in one constant rhythm round and round. If you want to sense their state of consciousness take a warm-up lap in the opposing direction on the track (stay to the far outside) and look at their facial expressions, sense their pleasure or effort. True, some may be "stuck" beautifully into the experience. But it becomes increasingly difficult if you are running the same sequence repeatedly—far better to be running at half efforts over short distances, gliding, and feeling the kinesthetic pleasures. Running to the top of a sand dune in the open air is different than running track laps. The aim is a quality, sense experience that is also a shortcut to physiological improvement.

The trail you use for LSD would ideally begin at your front door. It should be flat, and it would be helpful if it had a soft surface to it. This produces less jarring on the legs and back. Wear training shoes that are of medium weight and bend, so you can use them for speed work on the track and endurance on the road. The road should measure a route suited to the longest distance of anyone in your group or family. Others can run their distances out and back over the same route. Take notice and measure of telephone poles or other markings along the road. These can be used in your fartlek training. Besides these poles you can use a wristwatch to time segments. In the early training, your changes from day to day or your state may vary. The fartlek segments at that time may be the most difficult for you to master though your workout may call for a 1½ minute interval. If you can only manage 45 seconds, listen to your body response rather than following the planned workout.

Especially in the first two weeks, much long, slow running will be accomplished. This can be done according to time or distance. After a while you will have set courses which you are sure you can cover in certain amounts of time. At the beginning, the shortest time someone will be out is 8 minutes. This will be both shuffling and walking. The aim will be to eventually accomplish the 8 minutes in a shuffle without stopping to walk. In these runs sometimes it is better to run at a style of movement that is somewhere between a shuffle and a fresh swing. Don't be self-conscious about technique. Use the talk test (the ability to talk to yourself out loud or your neighbor) to make sure you are not running too fast. In LSD there really is no way of going too slowly. Practice mind-awareness techniques or run in a group, as this will constitute 65 percent of your early running. This 65 percent is a quota of time, distance, and effort.

I have given you an outline of the elements of a training program, and reasons for their use. You now have tools from which to shift from jogging to running. You know the swing tempos, how to shake-up, the way to run long and far in a shuffle. You know that there are many forms, many methods to improving physical functioning—intervals, fartlek running, speed work, resistance training. Each will help a lot, and even if you go on jogging, this information will make you think, and possibly change—and that is a beginning.

Before you begin the program familiarize yourself with the following:

Shuffle: landing far back on the heel with awareness focused below the knee.

Fresh swing tempo: lifting the knee, stepping out in a cyclical motion while being aware of the natural foot plant on the outside of the foot. Using this motion to roll off the outside of the foot, the tempo should be run between twenty and forty percent of your full potential.

Tidal breathing: techniques to utilize breathing to propel the body forward.

Good speed: resting from the natural movement by landing behind the toes (ball of the foot), and changing arm action to a balancer and rhythm-maker.

Shake-up to finish warm-up or after workout to let all the muscles hang on the skeleton like a rag doll while shaking as you are moving.

Surge: using the hands to focus concentration, coupled with throat sounds to propel the body forward.

Power run: a simulation of resistance running using the body against itself for muscle/skeletal strengthening.

Good swing tempo: same motion as fresh swing tempo but at 40 percent to 80 percent effort. Faster tempos are sprints.

Sprint form process: a four-part build-up while warming up that combines visualized movement with postured style to enable the body to maintain correct form while tiring in a sprint.

Canter: asymmetrical motion that is the end result of stretch, amble and trot in naturalistic running. *Gallop* is the same with more extended movements.

You will also find it useful to have some means of noting times for your runs. A stopwatch is ideal, but a wristwatch with a second hand will serve just as well.

LONG, SLOW DISTANCE (LSD) is the form in which you build up your endurance. It is accomplished by running long and slow either on a road or, if you insist, on a track. It builds primarily endurance and aerobic strength. LSD should always remain 50 percent of your training. It builds a base from which you can chisel out the rest of your training.

INTERVAL RUNNING. By breaking a distance into segments, you can increase your physical fitness. Intervals are to balance out the amount of aerobic and anaerobic metabolism. They also let you change the style of movement with which you are running. Play with your breath and the track stadium. Don't be afraid to stop for a while, run a bit faster for a time. Go to the track with a pre-planned workout, and other times make it up as you go along.

FARTLEK, SPEED PLAY. The freedom to run when you want to, in the way and pace that you choose, is a gateway to self-reliant running. Be spontaneous in a beautiful surrounding, if it is possible. Pick a time and spend that entire time out, but run in whatever way you choose.

SPEED. Even if you are not fast, you can improve your general conditioning quite a bit by running quickly for short periods. This has been proven by laboratory research, so take advantage. Short sprints that don't hurt very much can greatly improve your shape.

RESISTANCE running is for strength and spirit. You can build up a high-level anaerobic condition going up hill, and strengthen the legs also. Sometimes abandoning yourself to a hill is a purifying discipline. You don't have to be maniacal, but surrendering to a hill every now and again can be spiritually uplifting.

TIME ASSESSMENT. The need to do task-specific training—the condensing of methods into an actual experience—brings great joy and a feeling of accomplishment. It takes time for the body to adjust to this "putting together" of metabolic functioning. You will be surprised how you will jump to various levels and plateaus if you test yourself at intermediate times.

Helpful Hints

There are a number of hints that can make running more enjoyable. This pleasure comes from working in unison with the natural flow of the body. In most cases these practical questions have arisen many times in workshops or lectures I have delivered.

SURFACES

The ideal surface to run on would be even, cut grass. There are very few places where the grass is cut even enough for extensive workouts, even in places like California and Hawaii. For your interval workouts the grass around a stadium should be adequate, but for long running, and fartlek training an analysis of the road surfaces is necessary. Most country roads have a dirt shoulder or berm which can take a lot of the jarring out of long distance running. Many top long distance runners train almost exclusively on cement roads. Their justification is that these surfaces are even, and don't force the knee, foot and ankle to torque on each step forward. Many times you can find dirt roads in various places—along waterfronts, in parks, even next to railroad tracks. It is important to have trails that you can run to just out of your house, if it is possible. But, a drive occasionally to a track, seacoast, or hill is worth the effort.

TIMES TO RUN

Probably the best time to run is at noon. Many top long distance runners train twice a day, once in the early morning and again at evening. If you are committed to a normal work day the time it takes to get over the euphoria of the run may make the total time too long in the morning. For others, running in the morning precedes the necessary cleaning and washing that you would do anyway. If you wait for noon you can get the benefit of not being tired out from the day, but able to gain from the metabolic workings of the day's activities. A run before supper can allow you to make the transition from the day into the relaxed time of the evening.

SHOES

Runners are sometimes like Eskimos in that they have a shoe for every occasion. A shoe for long running, one for speed training, and another for racing. I have a shoe for races from three to eight miles and another from eight miles to the marathon, a spiked shoe for distance races and one for long races and cross-country. Many shoes on the market are overpriced and don't allow for a variety of training purposes in one shoe. Some of the best I have found are the Nike Oregon Waffle trainers, New Balance 320, Puma 9190, Easy Rider, the Nike LD1000 (mostly for roads), and the Tiger Jayhawk.

CLOTHING

Don't wear rubber suits, or any garment that makes you sweat artificially. The best way to dress is in layers of clothes. Shorts, sweat pants, and sweat shirt, a hood in cold weather. You can peel off layers when you find it necessary.

INJURIES

The rule of thumb on most injuries is that if they persist after you have begun running, or begin to become worse, you should not run. In the case of colds or flu it is best to completely rest for a few days and then begin again by walking, and gradually getting back into running.

For a more extensive view of diagnosis and symptoms of injuries, books like *Doctor Sheehan On Running* by George Sheehan should be consulted. Always remember that a good dose of stretching and awareness meditation adds tremendously to balancing out the tightness of muscles that occurs from running.

The Program

Before Beginning the Six-Week Program

... you will need to do a 5-day pre-training within which you will assess your present state of physical fitness.

To begin, estimate the level for which you would expect to qualify.

	A one mile distance in
Level I	12-15 minutes (or longer)
Level II	10-12 minutes
Level III	8-10 minutes
Level IV	6:45-8 minutes
Level V	5:30-6:45 minutes
Level VI	4:30-5:30 minutes

On the first day of the pre-training run one-half of the LSD workout from the level you choose. On the second day, run one-third of the interval workout for your estimated level. On the third day, rest.

On your assessment day run a mile, four laps around a standard 440-yard track, at 70 percent of your maximum effort. You won't actually know how to gauge effort, so begin moderately, and in the last lap and a half allow yourself to push a bit. If you decide to run for six minutes, it is easiest to run on a 440-yard track; convert the distance to a mile in order to determine your time for the

48

mile. For example, 2½ laps in six minutes would be equal to a mile in 9.6 minutes; mathematically, divide the number of laps (2.5) into 24 (six minutes times four laps); this time would qualify you for Level III.

Distances not run on a track will require careful estimates, if possible, using an automobile odometer. Use the estimated distance to calculate your time.

Take an additional easy day before beginning the program.

Aerobic/Anaerobic

At the beginning of the *Interval* workouts for each level, I have indicated the overall distance to be run, as well as the effort required in terms of aerobic/anaerobic ratio.

You never run at a level that is entirely aerobic or anaerobic. The aerobic state is one in which your body is utilizing the oxygen breathed in, and that oxygen is *sufficient* to meet the demands of a particular workout.

The anaerobic state is reached when you are running/working hard enough to produce a *deficit* of oxygen. You are calling on the muscles' reserves to provide the energy needed; the oxygen taken in can't supply all of the body's needs.

"Calling the Distance"

The core of fartlek running is spontaneity. When you have a workout that calls for "calling the distance," begin the run at a shuffle and begin spontaneously picking out markers, such as trees, telephone poles, rocks or buildings at which you will run anywhere from 20 to 80 percent effort. You can also run for a specific time period.

The chart below indicates the workout for each day. The pages following list the different workouts by level. Good luck!

THE SIX-WEEK PROGRAM

1 Interval 1	2 Rest	3 LSD 1	4 LSD/Fartlek	5 Rest	6 Speed	7 LSD 1
8 Rest	9 LSD/Resistance	10 Fartlek	11 Rest	12 Interval/Speed	13 LSD 1	14 Interval 1
15 Rest	16 LSD/Fartlek	17 Speed	18 LSD 1	19 Rest	20 Warm-up and Assessment	21 Interval 2
22 Resistance	23 Rest	24 Speed	25 LSD 2	26 Fartlek	27 Rest	28 Warm-up and Assessment
29 LSD 2	30 Interval 2	31 Rest	32 LSD/Resistance	33 LSD/Fartlek	34 Rest	35 Warm-up and Assessment
36 LSD 2	37 Interval/Speed	38 Rest	39 Interval 2	40 Fartlek	41 Rest	42 Warm-up and Assessment

LEVEL I

Interval 1 (1,280 yards)
    Easy to moderate effort
    80/20 percent aerobic/anaerobic

    Three minutes shuffle
    Four 50-yard shake-ups
    Two 60-yard fresh swing (walk or shuffle back to start)
    Two 80-yard—60 fresh swing/20 surge
    One 110-yard—60 fresh swing/50 tidal breathing
    Four 50-yard shake-ups

LSD 1—First Three Weeks
    Twelve minutes shuffle/walk

LSD 2—Second Three Weeks
    Eighteen minutes shuffle/walk/fresh swing

LSD/Fartlek
    Three minutes shuffle
    Five 20-second intervals at fresh swing, build to 30
        percent effort
    Two 100-yard—50 fresh swing/50 tidal breathing

    Shuffle or walk between intervals until fully recovered

Speed
    Three minutes shuffle
    Four 40-yard sprint form
    Four 50-yard shake-ups
    Three 60-yard—build to 70 percent at good swing

    Take as much rest as needed between intervals

LSD/Resistance

Six minutes shuffle/walk (if necessary)
Two 80-yard—paved or dirt hill of about 30° slant
OR
Three flights of stairs (about 30 feet vertically)
OR
Four 30-yard power runs

Fartlek

Ten minutes of calling the distance

Resistance

30-yard runs up a slope, sand dune or hill (if available), of more than 30°. Drive with arms low, making any sounds you wish. Run until somewhat exhausted.

Interval 2—After First Two Weeks (2,000 yards)

Easy to moderate effort
80/20 percent aerobic/anaerobic

Three minutes shuffle
Four 50-yard shake-ups
Three 80-yard fresh swing (walk or shuffle back to start)
Two 110-yard—60 fresh swing/50 tidal breathing
Two 150-yard—130 fresh swing/20 surge
Four 50-yard shake-ups

Interval/Speed

Two minutes shuffle
Four 50-yard shake-ups
Two 60-yard—build to canter (stretch, amble, trot)
Two 80-yard—60 fresh swing/20 surge
Two 60-yard—build to 70 percent good swing
Four 50-yard shake-ups

Warm-up for Assessments
Four minutes shuffle
Four 50-yard shake-ups

Assessments
Day 20—660 yards or one-third of the distance covered in the six-minute pre-test, at 70 percent (you may walk if necessary)
Day 28—100 yards at 90 percent effort
Day 35—1,320 yards at 80 percent effort or two-thirds of the distance covered in six-minute pre-test (you may walk if necessary)
Day 42—One mile at 90 percent effort or six minutes

Make-up Workout 1—First Two Weeks
One minute shuffle
Four 50-yard shake-ups
Three 60-yard fresh swing
Four-minute shuffle/walk

Make-up Workout 2—Second Two Weeks
Six minutes shuffle/walk
Four 50-yard shake-ups
Two 110-yard—60 good swing/50 fresh swing
Two 50-yard shake-ups

Make-up Workout 3—Final Two Weeks
Eighteen minutes shuffle/walk/fresh swing

LEVEL II

Interval 1 (2,000 yards)
    Easy to moderate effort
    80/20 percent aerobic/anaerobic

    Three minutes shuffle
    Four 50-yard shake-ups
    Three 80-yard fresh swing (walk or shuffle back to
        start)
    Two 110-yard—60 fresh swing/50 tidal breathing
    Two 150-yard—130 fresh swing/20 surge
    Four 150-yard shake-ups

LSD 1—First Three Weeks
    18-minute shuffle/walk/fresh swing

LSD 2—Second Three Weeks
    25-minute shuffle/fresh swing

LSD/Fartlek
    Five minutes shuffle/fresh swing
    Six 30-second intervals at fresh swing, build to 30
        percent effort
    Four 100-yard—50 fresh swing/50 tidal breathing

    Shuffle or walk between intervals until fully recovered

Speed
    Five minutes shuffle/fresh swing
    Four 50-yard shake-ups
    Four 50-yard sprint form
    Three 80-yard—build to 80 percent at good swing
    Four 50-yard shake-ups

LSD/Resistance
>   Eight minutes shuffle/fresh swing
>   Three 110-yard—paved or dirt hill of about 30° slant
>   OR
>   Four flights of stairs (about 40 feet vertically)
>   OR
>   Four 30-yard power runs

Fartlek
>   15 minutes of calling the distance

Resistance
>   30-yard runs up a slope, sand dune or hill (if available), of more than 30°. Drive with arms low, making any sounds you wish. Run until somewhat exhausted.

Interval 2—After First Two Weeks (2,560 yards)
>   Moderate effort
>   75/25 percent aerobic/anaerobic
>
>   Four minutes shuffle
>   Four 80-yard shake-ups
>   Three 110-yard fresh swing (walk or shuffle back to start)
>   Two 150-yard—100 fresh swing/50 tidal breathing
>   Two 260-yard good swing
>   Four 60-yard shake-ups

Interval/Speed
>   Three minutes shuffle
>   Four 50-yard shake-ups
>   Three 80-yard—build to canter (stretch, amble, trot)
>   Two 110-yard—60 fresh swing/50 tidal breathing
>   Two 80-yard—build to 80 percent good swing
>   Four 50-yard shake-ups

Warm-up for Time Assessment
    Four minutes shuffle/walk
    Four 50-yard shake-ups

Assessments
    Day 20—660 yards or one-third the distance covered in six-minute pre-test
    Day 28—100 yards at 90 percent effort
    Day 35—1,320 yards at 80 percent or two-thirds of the distance covered in six-minute pre-test
    Day 42—One mile at 90 percent effort at six minutes

Make-up Workout 1—First Two Weeks
    Three minutes shuffle
    Four 50-yard shake-ups
    Four 50-yard—one shuffle, three fresh swing, and minimal rest between intervals
    Five minutes shuffle

Make-up Workout 2—Second Two Weeks
    Nine minutes shuffle/fresh swing
    Four 50-yard shake-ups
    Two 150-yard—80 good swing/70 fresh swing
    Two 50-yard shake-ups

Make-up Workout 3—Final Two Weeks
    25 minutes shuffle/fresh swing

LEVEL III

Interval 1 (2,560 yards)
  Moderate effort
  75/25 percent aerobic/anaerobic

  Four minutes shuffle
  Four 80-yard shake-ups
  Three 110-yard fresh swing (walk or shuffle back to
    start)
  Two 150-yard—100 fresh swing/50 tidal breathing
  Two 260-yard good swing
  Four 60-yard shake-ups

LSD 1—First Three Weeks
  Twenty-five minutes shuffle/fresh swing

LSD 2—Second Three Weeks
  Thirty minutes shuffle/fresh swing

LSD/Fartlek
  Seven minutes shuffle/fresh swing
  Five 45-second intervals at fresh swing, build to 40
    percent effort
  Five 100-yard—50 fresh swing/50 tidal breathing

  Shuffle or walk between intervals until fully recovered

Speed
  Seven minutes shuffle/fresh swing
  Four 50-yard shake-ups
  Four 50-yard sprint form
  Three 90-yard—build to 70 percent at good swing
  Four 50-yard shake-ups

LSD/Resistance
>Thirteen minutes shuffle/fresh swing
>Three 150-yard—paved or dirt hill of about 30° slant
>OR
>Five flights of stairs (about 50 feet vertically)
>OR
>Five 30-yard power runs

Fartlek
>20 minutes calling the distance

Resistance
>30-yard runs up a slope, sand dune or hill (if available), of more than 30°. Drive with arms low, making any sounds you wish.
>Run until fairly exhausted.

Interval 2—After First Two Weeks (4,260 yards)
>Moderate effort
>70/30 percent aerobic/anaerobic

>Five minutes shuffle
>Four 100-yard shake-ups
>Four 110-yard swing (walk or shuffle back to start)
>Two 150-yard—100 fresh swing/50 tidal breathing
>One 330-yard—200 fresh swing/30 good speed/100 good swing
>Two 110-yard—90 fresh swing/20 surge
>Four 100-yard shake-ups

Interval/Speed
>Four minutes shuffle
>Four 80-yard—good swing
>Three 110-yard—build to canter (stretch, amble, trot)
>Two 150-yard—100 fresh swing/50 tidal breathing
>Two 90-yard good swing—build to 70 percent
>Four 80-yard shake-ups

Warm-up for Assessments
    Four minutes shuffle
    Four 50-yard shake-ups

Assessments
    Day 20—660 yards or one-third the distance covered
       in six-minute pre-test, at 70 percent
    Day 28—100 yards at 90 percent
    Day 35—1,320 yards at 80 percent or two-thirds the
       distance covered in six-minute pre-test
    Day 42—One mile at 90 percent effort or six minutes

Make-up Workout 1—First Two Weeks
    Four minutes shuffle
    Four 50-yard shake-ups
    Four 50-yard—one shuffle/3 fresh swing (back to
       back with no rest)
    Five minutes shuffle

Make-up Workout 2—Second Two Weeks
    Thirteen minutes shuffle/fresh swing
    Four 50-yard shake-ups
    Two 300-yard—200 good swing/100 fresh swing
    Two 50-yard shake-ups

Make-up Workout 3—Final Two Weeks
    30 minutes shuffle/fresh swing

LEVEL IV

Interval 1 (4,260 yards)
   Moderate effort
   70/30 percent aerobic/anaerobic

   Five minutes shuffle
   Four 100-yard shake-ups
   Four 110-yard fresh swing (walk or shuffle back to
      start)
   Two 150-yard—100 fresh swing/50 tidal breathing
   One 330-yard—200 fresh swing/30 good speed/100
      good swing
   Two 110-yard—90 fresh swing/20 surge
   Four 100-yard shake-ups

LSD 1—First Three Weeks
   30 minutes fresh swing

LSD 2—Second Three Weeks
   35 minutes fresh swing

LSD/Fartlek
   Ten minutes shuffle/fresh swing
   Five fresh swing—1 minute each, build to 40 percent
      effort
   Six 100-yard—50 fresh swing/50 tidal breathing

Speed
   Seven minutes shuffle/fresh swing
   Four 50-yard shake-ups
   Four 50-yard sprint form
   Three 100-yard—build to 80 percent at good swing
   Four 50-yard shake-ups

LSD/Resistance

Fifteen minutes fresh swing at 20 percent
Four 150-yard—paved or dirt hill of about 30° slant
OR
Five flights of stairs (about 50 feet vertically)
OR
Six 30-yard power runs

Fartlek

25 minutes calling the distance

Resistance

30-yard runs up a slope, sand dune or hill (if
available), of more than 30°. Drive with arms low,
making any sounds you wish. Run until somewhat
exhausted.

Interval 2—After First Two Weeks (5,340 yards)

Moderate effort
65/35 percent aerobic/anaerobic

Five minutes shuffle
Four 100-yard shake-ups
Three 150-yard—100 fresh swing/50 tidal breathing
(walk or shuffle back to start)
Two 260-yard—100 fresh swing/30 good speed/130
good swing
Two 330-yard—300 fresh swing/30 surge
Four 110-yard—60 fresh swing/50 good swing
Four 100-yard shake-ups

Interval/Speed

Five minutes shuffle
Four 100-yard shake-ups
Four 110-yard—build to canter (stretch, amble, trot)
Two 150-yard—100 fresh swing/50 tidal breathing
Two 100-yard—build to 80 percent good swing
Four 100-yard shake-ups

Warm-up for Time Assessment
　　Four minutes shuffle/walk
　　Four 50-yard shake-ups

Assessments
　　Day 20—660 yards or one-third the distance covered in six-minute pre-test, at 70 percent
　　Day 28—100 yards at 90 percent
　　Day 35—1,320 yards at 80 percent or two-thirds of the distance covered in six-minute pre-test
　　Day 42—One mile at 90 percent effort or six minutes

Make-up Workout 1—First Two Weeks
　　Five minutes shuffle/fresh swing
　　Four 50-yard shake-ups
　　Four 70-yard—three fresh swing/one good swing (back to back with no rest)
　　Seven minutes shuffle/fresh swing

Make-up Workout 2—Second Two Weeks
　　Fifteen minutes fresh swing at 20 percent
　　Four 50-yard shake-ups
　　Two 330-yard—260 good swing/70 fresh swing
　　Four 50-yard shake-ups

Make-up Workout 3—Final Two Weeks
　　35 minutes fresh swing

LEVEL V

Interval 1 (5,340 yards)
Moderate effort
65/35 percent aerobic/anaerobic

Five minutes shuffle
Four 100-yard shake-ups
Three 150-yard—100 fresh swing/50 tidal breathing
(walk or shuffle back to start)
Two 260-yard—100 fresh swing/30 good speed/
130 good swing
Two 330-yard—300 fresh swing/30 good swing
Four 110-yard—60 fresh swing/50 good swing
Four 100-yard shake-ups

LSD 1—First Three Weeks
35 minutes fresh swing

LSD 2—Second Three Weeks
45 minutes fresh swing

LSD/Fartlek
Twelve minutes fresh swing at 20 percent
Five fresh swing—1½ minutes each, hold to 40 percent
Five 100-yard—50 fresh swing/50 tidal breathing

Speed
Eight minutes fresh swing
Four 50-yard shake-ups
Four 50-yard sprint form
Four 110-yard good swing, build to 80 percent
Four 50-yard shake-ups

LSD/Resistance
Eighteen minutes fresh swing at 20 percent
Five 150-yard—paved or dirt hill of about 30° slant
OR
Six flights of stairs (about sixty feet vertically)
OR
Six 30-yard power runs

Fartlek
   28 minutes calling the distance

Resistance
   30-yard runs up a slope, sand dune or hill (if available), of more than 30°. Drive with arms low, making any sounds you wish. Run until somewhat exhausted.

Interval 2—After First Two Weeks (6,280 yards)
   Moderate effort
   65/35 percent aerobic/anaerobic

   Five minutes shuffle
   Four 100-yard shake-ups
   Four 110-yard fresh swing (walk or shuffle back to start)
   Three 220-yard—100 fresh swing/20 good speed/100 good swing
   One 330-yard—300 fresh swing/30 surge
   Four 260-yard—150 fresh swing/110 tidal breathing
   Four 100-yard shake-ups

Interval/Speed
   Five minutes shuffle
   Four 100-yard shake-ups
   Three 110-yard—build to canter (stretch, amble, trot)
   Two 260-yard—100 fresh swing/30 good speed/130 good swing
   Three 110-yard—build to 80 percent at good swing
   Four 100-yard shake-ups

Warm-up for Assessment
   Four minutes shuffle/fresh swing
   Four 50-yard shake-ups

Assessments
   Day 20—660 yards or one-third the distance covered in six-minute pre-test, at 70 percent
   Day 28—100 yards at 90 percent effort

Day 35—1,320 yards at 80 percent effort or two-thirds
the distance covered in six-minute pre-test
Day 42—One mile at 90 percent effort or six minutes

Make-up Workout 1—First Two Weeks
Six minutes shuffle/fresh swing
Four 50-yard shake-ups
Four 80-yard good swing (back to back with no rest)
Eight minutes shuffle

Make-up Workout 2—Second Two Weeks
Eighteen minutes shuffle/fresh swing
Four 50-yard shake-ups
Two 360-yard—280 good swing/80 fresh swing
Four 50-yard shake-ups

Make-up Workout 3—Final Two Weeks
45 minutes fresh/good swing

LEVEL VI

Interval 1 (6,280 yards)
    Moderate effort
    65/35 percent aerobic/anaerobic

    Five minutes shuffle
    Four 100-yard shake-ups
    Four 110-yard fresh swing (walk or shuffle back to
        start)
    Three 220-yard—100 fresh swing/20 good speed/100
        good swing
    One 330-yard—300 fresh swing/30 surge
    Four 260-yard—150 fresh swing/110 tidal breathing
    Four 100-yard shake-ups

LSD 1—First Three Weeks
    45 minutes fresh swing

LSD 2—Second Three Weeks
    60 minutes fresh/good swing

LSD/Fartlek
    Fifteen minutes fresh swing
    Four fresh swing—1½ minutes each, build to 40
        percent effort
    Three 300-yard—100 fresh swing/30 good speed/re-
        mainder good swing

Speed
    Eight minutes fresh/good swing
    Four 80-yard shake-ups
    Four 50 yard sprint form
    Four 150-yard—build to 90 percent
    Four 80-yard shake-ups

LSD/Resistance
    Twenty-two minutes fresh swing at 30 percent
    Six 150-yard—paved or dirt hill of about 30° slant
    OR
    Seven flights of stairs (about 70 feet vertically)
    OR
    Seven 30-yard power runs

Fartlek
    30 minutes calling the distance

Resistance
    30-yard runs up a slope, sand dune or hill (if available), of more than 30°. Drive with arms low, making any sounds you wish. Run until somewhat exhausted.

Interval 2—After First Two Weeks (9,840 yards)
    Moderate to hard effort
    60/40 percent aerobic/anaerobic

    Five minutes shuffle
    Four 100-yard shake-ups
    Three 220-yard—100 fresh swing/20 good speed/100 good swing
    Three 330-yard—300 good swing/30 surge
    Four 110-yard fresh swing
    Four 260-yard fresh swing
    Four 260-yard—150 good swing/110 tidal breathing
    Four 100-yard shake-ups

Interval/Speed
    Five minutes shuffle
    Four 100-yard shake-ups
    Three 150-yard build to canter (stretch, amble, trot)
    Two 330-yard good swing
    Three 150-yard—build to 90 percent
    Four 100-yard shake-ups

Warm-up for Assessments
    Four minutes shuffle/walk
    Four 50-yard shake-ups

Assessment
    Day 20—660 yards or one-third the distance covered
        in six-minute pre-test, at 70 percent
    Day 28—100 yards at 90 percent effort
    Day 35—1,320 yards at 80 percent or two-thirds the
        distance covered in six-minute pre-test
    Day 42—One mile at 90 percent effort or six minutes

Make-up Workout 1—First Two Weeks
    Seven minutes shuffle/walk
    Four 50-yard shake-ups
    Four 80-yard good swing (back to back with no rest)
    Eight minutes shuffle

Make-up Workout 2—Second Two Weeks
    Twenty-two minutes shuffle/fresh swing
    Four 50-yard shake-ups
    Two 400-yard—330 good swing/70 fresh swing
    Four 50-yard shake-ups

Make-up Workout 3—Final Two Weeks
    60 minutes fresh swing/good speed

Short Form

The short form of the six-week program is not just for people who don't have the time for a detailed schedule. It is also for those who want or who need more freedom in their daily regimen. At any rate, it is the principles of the program which are the most essential, not the specific schedule.

When setting up your own schedule it is necessary to think in two-week cycles. With all the elements it takes to put together an overall program, a week's planning just won't allow all the necessary aspects. I will tell you what went on in my mind as I was setting up the long form of this six-week program and perhaps you can extrapolate from this information to construct your own program.

As much as possible, follow the charts, and do the workout outlined for each day. In some cases you may want to do your own version or otherwise change the workouts. This is okay in certain situations. Especially if you have experience through previous running programs. Remember that this sequence of workouts is designed for the mile run, and that the balance between the various methods has this as its premise.

The first two weeks—If you have done a mile or a six-minute effort you will have some indication of your current fitness level. Look over the long form of the six-week program to see what kinds of workouts people in your particular category are doing. If you don't have a category from an assessment, gauge what your time might be, and look over that part of the chart.

In the first two weeks it is important to spend an adequate amount of time on your legs. You shouldn't strain in the first two weeks, but get your body used to the amount of effort needed. The initial build-up is done in the first two weeks. You want intervals that give you a little anaerobic endurance, but more importantly, intervals in which you can sense and feel fluidity rather than fatigue. You want long, slow running to get you in the mood for being in shape. You want to play with the tempos; see how your body responds to finding its own levels of effort. In fartlek practice, what is 20 percent and what is 60 percent of your effort? In beginning fartlek, you can also practice the running techniques at your own leisure.

The first two weeks are a time to test your speed. You needn't take all-out leaps into being a "speed merchant," but see how it feels to sprint, and do it for less than 15 seconds. Resistance work is not so important in the first two weeks. It is best to stay on flat roads, and be moderate with intervals and speed work.

In the second two-week period the tempo begins to increase. You should do one time assessment like the 660 which appears in the long form. It is mainly a time to gather your endurance, increase the amount of intervals, do some running up hills, and burst a bit more into the speed work rather than easing into it. An important thing in this second two-week period is to gauge the amount of rest needed in comparison to the running. You want to rest your legs before speed work, carry on in the LSD even if you don't feel fresh. Increase the volume of the intervals.

The second two-week period will be one of self-investigation. At times you will not feel so new or spry during a workout. The rewards will come in smaller dosages, and keeping to the complexity of workouts—intervals, fartlek, speed, resistance—will at times seem a bother. You will have the tendency to want to go out and just run. Sometimes if you have this urge, do it. You are not necessarily hooked into the six-week schedule, and if you have made the choice for your freedom, use it. The detailed schedule is just a guide. All I am asking you to do is to be aware that you get in shape quicker by breaking a distance up and running faster, going as fast as you can for a short period of time, running up hills, resting appropriately and giving yourself short tests over the final distance you want to accomplish.

The third two-week period is a time of sharpening, and zoning in. In the long form there is a rather strenuous time assessment at ¾ of a mile. Keep in mind that if you are aiming at accomplishing a certain feat, the body has to practice putting the elements together. I remember lots of runners who would put in the miles, and some intervals and never quite get it all together. Remember that a world-class miler might run two hours a day and have to condense his training into a 4-minute effort. Many coaches claim this transition is one of the most difficult.

Auxiliary Tools

The purpose of these tools is not as a substitute for the actual training, but as a means of maintaining fitness when it is impossible to achieve normal workout conditions: You may be stuck in a hotel room; or unable to leave a young baby; sometimes people are stuck in highrise apartment buildings. For these people the necessity of substitute methods of conditioning are necessary. These exercises are only a stopgap, and should never be used in place of the planned training.

Running in place can be a helpful way to *maintain* a level of fitness you are in the process of developing. You can run in place every morning before you take a shower. Stand on something soft like a carpet and run in place. Bring your knees up about one third of the way. An absolute beginner can start by running in place for 15 seconds daily, and each succeeding day add five seconds.

There are variations to running in place which can be done in a small space. First, while running in a fixed spot, lift your knees up to your chest with your hands on your hips. This exercises the stomach muscles as well as strengthens the legs.

Another running supplement is to take the length of a room, ideally a living room of good size, and see how many steps you can take in that amount of space. Small, little steps, hitting the ground very quickly and lightly as if you were treading on eggs. This can cause a very quick anaerobic oxygen debt.

Another exercise which was one of Cerutty's favorite auxiliary tools: Bend over and take air into your lungs as you are straightening up. When you come upward with full lungs, stamp the feet, make a sound deep in your throat, and hop quickly on both feet, while making a "ping" sound in the throat.

The power run, as defined elsewhere can be used in short halls or in hotel corridors. In fact, it is amazing what you can do inside hotels. Recently I was at a conference in the Bonaventure Hotel in Los Angeles. The hotel is somewhat like a walled city, six floors, an outside deck and garden. I was able to complete an incredible workout running up and down the flights of stairs, and around each floor—one lap was about a half mile. Long hallways allowed 150-yard straightaways. A couple of runs around the place really was a workout. On my first lap I peeled off a sweat shirt which the security guards brought to the lost and found. There was a time when a jogger on the city street was sneered at, now people smile as I go by. The times have changed and there is no reason to feel embarrassment in performing a workout in unorthodox places and situations. Simply use commonsense and avoid those places where there may be danger, or your presence could be disruptive or annoying to others.

The sit-up is a vital tool for the back and stomach area. This is done by lying on your back with your feet flat on the floor, or hooked under a heavy piece of furniture. Put your hands behind your head, come up only one-third of the way. Breathe out as you come up and breathe in as you lower your upper body back to the floor. Start with five repetitions, add one a day until you are doing thirty repetitions.

Win Paris, a friend who is president of Super Fitness of America, adds a few stationary exercises in his book *Super Fitness*. He says, "If you sit all day in an office, I recommend you do about five shoulder shrugs an hour,

first going up, forward and down, and then up, backward and down. Also perform the hug and squeeze for the upper back. Begin by hugging yourself, then move your elbows back and squeeze your shoulder blades together. Perform five repetitions each hour."

Walk to your local store instead of taking the car. It will give you exercise and, if you have been training consistently, reduces lactic acid in the legs. Be careful lifting things. Lift with your back under the weight. Take up a sport in which you have an interest you have never pursued or one you might have had success at in your younger days. Add this about three weeks after you are into the training program.

Warm-Down Visualization

In the preceding chapters, I have presented various ways to improve and short-cut methods to physical fitness. There have been exercises to expand consciousness and heighten the spiritual purposes of our practices. One area of training that is given too little attention is the finish of the work-out, or warming down. Usually, to warm down physically, a person shuffles or does a series of shake-ups. With the added dimensions of innerspace exploration, there is also the necessity to slow the mind down. Consciousness practices can aid in the relaxing of muscles after exercise is completed.

Shake-ups bring the body to the remembrance of the feeling it had before the day's exercise. Shake-ups leave the body with a sense of relaxation. They allow you to savor and integrate the work-out into the flow of your training plan. I'd like to expand the idea of physical warm-down to include inner exploration and body awareness.

A warm down visualization may proceed as follows.

Keep your eyes focused downward so your mind does not drift. Walking slowly, begin by visualizing a light about the size of a halo over your head. Choose a color that comes to mind, and draw the colored light through your body. Take a series of breaths in and draw the colored light through your body. Take a series of breaths in and draw the light down as far as your neck, then expand it into your chest, and finally take a deep, refreshing breath all the way into your abdomen. On each exhalation let your body relax and allow another level of tension to leave your body. Next, repeat the breathing process, adding to the haloed light the image of a soothing smell. Draw the smell through your neck, chest, and down into your abdomen. Next picture in your mind a layer of warmth wrapped a few inches outside your legs. Let the sensation of warmth soothe and relax your muscles. Let the heat you feel around your legs go deep into the bone. Become aware of how and where your feet touch the ground as you walk. Shake your feet, relax them, and visualize a red light a few inches outside surrounding your foot, and on each step forward let the imagined light give an extra confidence as you take each step. Still walking slowly, focus on various areas of your body. Look at your feet, legs, back, knees. Anyplace where there is soreness or fatigue, give that area special attention by breathing in imagined menthol. Finish by walking easily a few steps.

Hopefully, this visualization will have enabled you to feel calmed, refreshed, rejuvenated and recovered.

On Stretching

In the last few years we have recognized the importance and necessity for incorporating flexibility systems into physical fitness programs, especially those which focus on running. This is because running, by its nature, stiffens muscles, and contracts them. Flexibility exercises lengthen them. Stretching of muscles helps to prevent ligament problems, stress fractures, and induces calmness and helps relaxation in your running.

Then, what kind of stretching should I do? I don't want to definitely answer this question for anyone—we all have different kinds of bodies. I will suggest some basic exercises, which flex the parts of the body tending to be overused in running, and those which by loosening will improve your body mechanically. Do these exercises once a day. Preferably before you run, or afterwards. A session just before bed is relaxing and will allow maximum stretches. If it is at all possible, seek out a teacher who can fill in any gaps you might find in my presentation as it applies to you.

First of all, stretching is not for show. It isn't how far you can bend over or what difficult positions you can get into. Stretching for running should be looked upon as insurance against injury. It is the counterbalance to running which, for the most part, constricts the muscles. This constriction is also true of musculoskeletal exercises which are also considered in this section. Stretching helps in keeping muscles toned, and flexible. Having these integrated with the running is important. It doesn't matter how well you do, it is the consistency that will give you the benefits. As Cerutty writes, "There is no special advantage in being able to touch your toes, or put your palms on the floor. All that indicates is that your joints lock late. With some people, their joints lock early. They can never really straighten out their extended arm, or leg, and when they bend over, find it difficult if not impossible to touch their toes."

The secret is consistency and finding the routine correct for what you need to accomplish, and working at it, "Putting in your chops," as my yoga teacher, Ken Dychtwald, says. There are basic exercises, but a lot of people "do the exercises that are easy for them and neglect the ones which could be really useful."

One form of stretching which is helpful is *Scandinavian Rhythmics*. The object of rhythmics is to combine stretching exercises with visualization, creating images that free the mind from concentration on the exercises to be accomplished. Rhythmics combine imaging with motion. Here are four you can do in your home.

1. While doing a stretch, reach up as though you are going to pull down the ceiling or sky. Picture yourself first pulling down the sky with all your might; then reaching to your fullest extension, push the sky upward.

2. Kneel, doubled over with your forehead touching the floor and extend your arms along your legs. Think of your body mass as small and as little as possible. Relax and think of yourself as a small seedling in the ground. Stay in this position for perhaps a minute or two while continuing to imagine yourself a seed.

Next, come out of this position. Slowly at first, picturing yourself as a flower beginning to blossom. Rise up slowly into early spring. Rise into full stretch in the early summer. Visualize yourself as a flower blooming in the warm midsummer and reach toward the sky, giving your body a full stretch.

3. Here is a rhythmic exercise for your lower back. Begin by swiveling your hips in a circle. Push out to the full radius of the circle. Next swing your arms in an arc from the ground as though throwing water over your shoulders. Visualize yourself throwing water over each shoulder.

4. Another exercise for your back: Picture yourself as a knight on a horse in a joust. Begin swirling from the hips as one would if you were swinging a long hammer with a spiked ball on the end. As you ride, swivel and throw the hammer. Let your body extend fully as you release.

The exercises that follow are some that I have developed or selected from other sources as being particularly helpful for me, and seemed to be the most generally beneficial for those I have worked with and taught. These exercises are for people with average ranges of flexibility. They are arranged in sets as a suggestion for the kinds of combinations that can be done.

SET I

1. *Bellows:* lift knees individually toward chest while lying on back; exhale 5 times and pull knee closer each time.

2. Lift each knee same as above; rotate in circular motion.

3. *Cobra:* push-up but with pelvis grounded (to stretch spine).

4. *Pelvis rotation:* circular motion while standing.

5. *Pelvis lift:* lie on back, arch small of back pushing stomach up, then slowly push pelvis up and push small of back against floor.

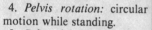

6. Swing arm, parallel to shoulders; rotate torso freely.

7. Throwing weight on a rope, circular arm motion overhead.

SET II

8. Circular arm swings, outstretched to side, making smaller and smaller circles.
9. Standing, breathe in, put fists up into chest, stretch up on toes.

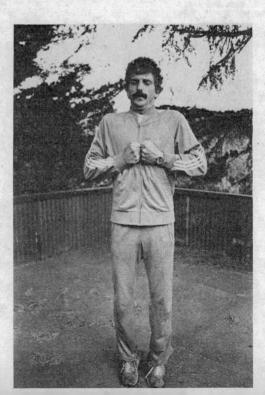

10. Lie on back, bend , lift over leg and touch floor on opposite side to stretch back and thigh muscles; repeat with other leg

11. *Meditation:* visualize feather going from forehead to ceiling and back.

12. *Bow:* reach back for ankles and raise chest while pulling towards the head.

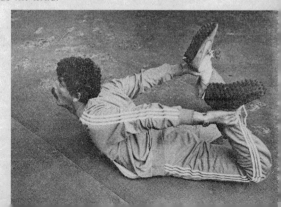

13. *Running on spot:* crouch over, fill lungs with air, stand up expelling air with "binggg…" sound and run in place as fast as you can before losing air.

14. *Pelvis lift:* Same as #5 (p.85)

15. On back, knees up to chest, roll pelvis and legs from side to side keeping shoulders flat.

16. Step out, stretch forward and over knee with arms uplifted.

SET III

17. Reach for grapes, stretching arms, feet, toes.
18. Swing arms in circles in front of body (not to side as in #6).
19. Left arm on left hip, other arm over head, lean left looking up; repeat on other side.

20. Pelvis rotation: same as #4.

21. Lie down, pull left leg out and back, press knee down toward floor. Be careful not to strain leg; repeat with other leg.

22. Lie on back, arms stretched overhead; push heels out, pull toes toward you, stretch.

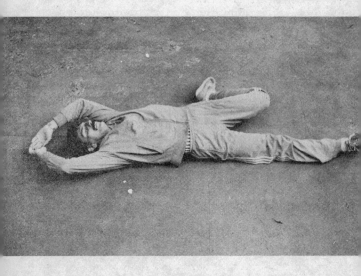

Feldenkrais Exercises

Moshe Feldenkrais is an Israeli who developed a form of body awareness that enabled him to overcome a crippling knee injury. A world-renowned judo expert, during the last forty years he has probed the relationship between experience and motor expression. He is the originator of a system of profound body awareness.

Dr. Feldenkrais lectures and teaches in the United States yearly. Many group leaders in the human potential movement have been influenced by his teachings. One of these is Will Schutz, an innovator in many fields of mind/body development:

The Feldenkrais approach to the body could revolution-ize all of athletics. Feldenkrais believes that if I strain, my body is not being used properly. My body will do everything it is capable of doing if I just learn to communicate with it. If I perform strenuously, I must fight myself to achieve that performance. If Feldenkrais were taken seriously, almost everything in athletics would change. The way we warm up, the way we exercise, the way we train, the achievement of flexibility, ideas about handedness, methods of learning complex movements, and the avoidance of injury would all change.

Feldenkrais claims that we use our bodies at such a low level of efficiency that virtually every movement we make is done by a small number of muscles with the others either not participating or actually opposing the move-ment. Strongly one-handed people exemplify this. The movement with the right arm, such as a tennis stroke, is usually actually inhibited by some of the muscles on the left side of the body. Feldenkrais' exercises are aimed at integrating all of the muscles of the body so that movement is made most gracefully and with the least effort.

Graceful movement is accomplished through the nervous system, where impulses are sent to the muscles with a certain rapidity and in a certain sequence. Feldy is saying that if we become aware of our bodies, we will function with far greater efficiency and with far less effort. This is true not only for movement, but also for other functions mediated by the nervous system—thinking, sensing and feeling.

Feldenkrais' view is that warm-up for physical activities is done best by never straining muscles, but rather by moving them, repeatedly, up to their limit. Muscles release when standard patterns are broken and movements occur which utilize the independence of each muscle. This method is far more effective than those requiring strain, such as push-ups, jumping jacks and other of the usual warming-up techniques.

Feldenkrais emphasizes body awareness. The key to avoiding injury and illness is awareness. Drawing on this fact, the approach to injury in athletic events would be reassessed. No longer would injured players be looked upon as suffering unfortunate accidents. The accidents are choices the players are making. Training in increased body/mind awareness would be used to minimize injury.

Let me present to you two Feldenkrais exercises to demonstrate this point. The first is taught by Will Schutz to dramatize the possibilities of breaking fixed mind/body interactions. The second is from a tape of Ruth Alon's, an Israeli who has studied extensively with Feldenkrais and teaches his method.

First, take your right hand, raise it in front of you and bring it back as far right as it will comfortably go. Let your head follow the lead of your arm and mark the spot of the greatest range of flexibility. Next, again swing your arm as far comfortably to the right as possible, but let your head go to the left. Do this movement five times.

Next, let your hand go again as far to the right as possible and let your eyes go to the left. Do this movement five times. You will find yourself in a position that you probably have never experienced before. When you again let your arm go to the right, and your head follow in the same direction, you will notice about 25 percent improvement in your range of movement. By breaking a fixed pattern you were able to increase your flexibility. Of course, this is beneficial for the arm socket and wouldn't be particularly useful for running, but it does demonstrate the Feldenkrais principle especially well.

Next, raise your left arm and bring it back as far as you can comfortably while looking to the right. Mark (or

note) the spot on the wall. Now do the exercises in your mind on the right as you did physically on the left. Remember the muscles that will pull, but follow the movement in your mind; let your head go to the opposite direction five times in your mind. When you do the exercise physically, lifting the left hand and bringing it back, you will see that the range of flexibility achieved in your mind is just about the same as when it is done physically.

The following exercise is part of a short lesson taught by Ruth Alon:

Lie flat on your back, your hands to the sides, thumbs pointing to the ceiling. Let the right hand slide a little bit away from the body, a very small movement.

Look to the left and duplicate the angle between your right hand and your body on the left; then, move the hand a little bit more to the left. Then alternate—look to the right and push the right hand a little bit more to the right; look to the left and push the left hand more to the left. Let your spine come down to the floor, you want to touch the floor with your spine.

Now, stop and notice how your back feels on the floor. Which part can you feel touching the floor that you didn't feel at the beginning of the exercise?

From the prone position, bring your knees to your chest, keep them apart, feet relaxed, head on the floor, hands to the side. Begin to raise the right hand above your head to the left so that all your body will turn on the left side, with right knee on top of the left knee, right hand on top of the left hand. Direct your body weight and energy toward your right hand as it moves in a circle above your head so that your body comes back to lie on the back; then repeat this on the left side. Move back and forth several times so that the right hand is leading the movement.

At the end of the last repetition remain on the left, with the legs bent. With the right leg bent, move it down so the right knee is over the left foot. Bring the right knee, still bent as it was, back on top of the left knee.

Lead with the right hand again in the circle above the head to the right. Come back to a position on the back with both knees on the chest and feet in the air. Now do it again. Begin the circle, turn on the right and as you turn continue the circle, leading with your right hand. Slide down the right knee as you continue the circle, lean on your elbow and sit up.

Bend forward at the waist so your head is above the left knee, your chest on top of the left knee, and slide both hands toward the left foot, head down. Leading with the right hand, circle back to the right and lie on your back.

Beginning from the body, draw the right knee to the stomach, then the left one. Circling to the left, draw your head down along the floor till it comes over the knee, then sit up; go back the same way. Lay your head over the knee—don't lean on the elbows, but right on the shoulder—and the right hand leading your body in a right circle takes you onto your back.

Take one knee above the other and then to the stomach. Now rest a moment, stretch out, and close your eyes. Try to observe the difference in feeling between right and left. What places in your body feel differently? Be aware of them, think about the length of your hands. . . .

Musculoskeletal Strength

We come finally to the question of musculoskeletal strength. Here there is a wide gap between the competitive athlete, especially the middle-distance runner, and the person seeking optimum health. In an overall program for the average person, flexibility should take priority over strength. If you have 30 minutes to practice you are going to get much more out of it by doing a cardiorespiratory exercise rather than a muscle-building routine, but there are some basic strengthening exercises which can help everyone.

When Cerutty lived with me in 1974, he was always talking about marketing a pully apparatus which would make strengthening exercises available in the home. At Portsea, Percy's camp, the weights are outside. People lift in the sunlight, then run up sand dunes.

In his book on general health, *Be Fit or Be Damned*, he says, "All muscular exercise constricts, or shortens the muscles used. It is necessary to counter this as one ages, to stretch all limbs, and the trunk, as does a cat, after resting. The most efficient, for humans, is to hang from a horizontal bar."

Another simple exercise that is often overlooked is sit-ups. Lie down on the floor, place feet under a piece of furniture, or something similar that will keep your feet down, and do daily sit-ups.

I am not going to stress weight training in our

program. It would be a good inclusion, but again the question of priorities, the consciousness aspects, learning new ways to run, and flexibility systems, I feel, must come first. There could be ways of beginning with light weights, working towards lifting just a few heavy weights a limited number of times for strength. There could be dead lifts that strengthen the muscles in the shoulders used for cantering and tidal breathing. But, it is too dangerous not knowing each one of you, to work out the individual mechanics.

Try the Feldenkrais exercise, go over the Scandinavian rhythmics, look over the exercises I recommend, discuss your problem with a fitness teacher. Then, three times a week for about twenty minutes set up a routine for yourself and do your chosen exercises as part of the six-week program.

Aston Patterning

One of the main problems with most analyses of running is that we pay too much attention to times, distances, and efforts, and not enough to style of movement. Judith Aston studies and understands movement. Her thesis is that we hold tension in various parts of our body, which restricts our potential movement. This causes injuries, and pain. By practicing exercises that make us aware of the way we move, calmness and grace can become part of our movement and life patterns.

Cerutty paid careful attention to the way runners move. Gunder Hagg, the famous Swede, ran hundreds of races, usually with outstanding times. Cerutty commented that his style wasted no movement: all motion was straight ahead, efficiency, grace. Experiments have been done with world-class athletes to determine the way in which their bodies operate. Many waste enormous amounts of effort in their movement. But, as Judith explains, the real process would be for them to find their ideal motion—a personal, not a universal thing.

Judith was originally a dancer and movement educator. She became a dance artist, teacher, and movement facilitator to the gestalt process. In her training and association with Dr. Ida Rolf, Judith was encouraged to focus on a more refined awareness of movement and its relationship to gravity. Her work helps people reclaim unused, unfamiliar spaces in their bodies which were crowded out by stress.

Judith, who has worked with me several times, discovered that my left foot goes out like a duck. This cuts down on my efficiency to push off the ground. She taught me to practice falling forward to help me find the correct lean of my body. In an Aston Patterning class the teacher helps you become aware of the way you are using your body and guides you to discover other, more agreeable ways of moving.

Judith explains her practice:

> You may be "holding on" to a belief, a lifestyle or a posture. You may be "holding down" your exuberance, your breath, or your head. You may be "holding out" for the perfect person, "holding back" your feelings. There are many ways of holding, many wheres and many whys. No matter how justified, these holding patterns demand effort. When unnecessary effort is repeated over and over, you begin to shape yourself into a stressed body which conflicts with who you really are. As you uncover patterns you may discover you have been wearing patterns that don't even belong to you but rather to someone else: a parent, a teacher, a coach.

I believe sports awareness is moving in the direction of Judith Aston's thought, and practice. If we are to move into an era of athletic experience in which pleasure, grace, efficiency, and form play the vital role in seeking self-gratification, faster timings, and a thorough examination of the body at work, our functional, emotional, and artistic nature must be examined and new kinds of preparation discovered—and a knowledge of Aston Patterning is a move in that direction.

By talking to Judith, and attending her classes over the last few years, I have come to realize it is not just learning subtle techniques to change the way you are moving, but looking internally to seek the sources of sometimes deeply ingrained habits. Once, as we were sitting talking, Judith stood up and explained, "Look at the way a person might move, pelvis out, hips forward, chest constricted, neck hunched. The knee problems start all the way back in the neck." I saw an image of a lot of us running down the road.

Breathing and the Lungs

When you are running full-out on a road it is often next to impossible to get an accurate understanding of how your lungs are functioning. We know we get out of breath, it is difficult to get enough air, the upper body becomes tense and movement becomes restricted.

Let's observe how the lungs usually function in high-level physical functioning. If you were to stand next to a running track and listen to top-class runners, you would be surprised at how many at the point of maximum fatigue breathe out rather than suck air in.

Try this: Blow air out from your lungs forcefully and notice what happens. Immediately the lungs suck in fresh air. So the primary concern when you are tired is not to gasp more new air in, but get rid of the old air inside.

Percy Cerutty's notions for full lung aeration are radical in track and field teaching, but someone like Magaur Proskauer, a noted expert on breathing, says the same thing in somewhat different terms. The capacity for the lungs is great, but exercises are not usually done to improve the functions of breathing. If we are to do breathing exercises only when under stress, such as after heavy physical exertion, the body does not automatically adopt the best possible response—these have to be learned.

Cerutty had a "crooked lung" and did not have the full capacity for breathing, therefore, he experimented with ways of getting full use of lung power. A few observations from his teachings show a lot. As with much of this work, it is with the novice, and you, the recreational athlete, that these techniques can be most successfully brought into use. Greater capacity to bring in fresh air is a benefit in itself. It need not have the added dimensions of helping you run faster times, although this may be a by-product.

The natural operation of the lungs is amazing. In a day's output, the lungs with their sponge-like substance, handle, wash, and reoxygenate 25 million red corpuscles. The lungs are made up of some 800 million air cells or alveoli. This tremendous capacity can be utilized by developing full use of the lungs. Full use is attained through experimentation with various ways of breathing, through the use of certain principles such as using your breath to propel yourself forward, working with understanding and becoming aware of how you breathe, and doing relaxation breathing exercises *separately* from your running. Full use of the lungs only comes from adventurous experiments with your breathing patterns, using the arms differently, concentrating on technique. Cerutty writes in *Be Fit or Be Damned*, "As organs, the apex of each lung extends into the neck area and above the collarbone, whilst the base, or bottom rests upon the diaphragm, that little-used membrane and which plays *the most important part in breathing*, a fact which is so little understood by civilized man, and curiously enough, with the techniques of running considered normal and natural, hardly used at all by most athletes!"

From my work and personal experimentation I have found out some important things about breathing that you may find useful. Sometimes raising the arms next to the chest rather than carrying the arms at the side can create an "elevator effect"; automatically, by raising the shoulders you can create greater atmospheric pressure that sucks in air. Remember, it is not the breath out that refreshes, but the clearing of the old air for the next draw of air in. Each breath need not be the same length or depth. Spontaneity and change in running pattern and breathing pattern is very often overlooked.

Try this breathing pattern and consequent visualization. Run near the ocean or picture yourself running near it. Draw air into your body by turning the palms outward and raising the shoulders take the air inside. Out of the corner of your eye look to the real or imagined ocean. Sense the cresting and breaking of a wave. When the wave breaks, turn the palm downward and expel the air—somewhat like the apparatus of an internal combustion engine. On the exhale propel yourself forward. Continue the momentum for a number of yards after the technique. See if you feel extra energy and have a feeling of distance covered without hard effort. This is called *Tidal Breathing*.

Long Distance Runners*

Some years ago the track coach was predominantly concerned with a group of relatively outstanding young male athletes. Recent social trends, and a realization that aerobic activities such as running have benefits to offer young people of all abilities and both sexes, have added a rather different group of people, young and older, to the fold, so that many physical educators must now consider what participation in aerobic sports has to offer to the large numbers of less-talented, or less dedicated people who pass through their hands, but who are not destined to be champions.

Of all the benefits of regular physical activity, the *psychological effects* are perhaps the least well understood, but the most rewarding in an increasingly stressful world. Post-exercise tranquility is well known to the exerciser, and provides an oasis of calm in the desert of a stressful week. It may well serve as a substitute for those other popular, temporary stress-relievers—alcohol and drugs. Far more work is needed in this important area.

Exercise brings about numerous physiological changes in the unconditioned human body. *Body composition* changes as a result of running and similar activities, muscle mass increasing somewhat, and fat decreasing. A group of middle-aged business men—who are also long-distance runners—was recently found by us to be virtually identical to large groups of young men in military training in mean body fat content (13 percent) and in several other anthropometric measures. Women runners—though showing a greater fat content than the active men—enjoyed a much lower fat level than their inactive female contemporaries.

The *heart* itself changes with aerobic exercise. It enlargers—but in a healthy way—to become a bigger, more powerful pump. The resting heart-rate slows; stroke volume increases. Muscle cells develop more mitochondria.

*Contributed by Peter D. Wood, D.Sc., Stanford Heart Disease Prevention Program

The arm and leg *muscles* change: their mitochondrial numbers increase, and so do enzyme levels of the muscle. The whole muscle system becomes more efficient, centrally and peripherally. A person who is in this well-conditioned state is much better placed than an unfit person to withstand abrupt physiological insults—an injury, or a sudden illness.

Blood pressure falls following vigorous exercise. Generally very active people have relatively low pressures, although the value of exercise in reducing elevated blood pressure is not very clear. But note that one of the first aims of a physician treating hypertension is to eliminate surplus body fat...which the very active person has already done.

Does running prevent *cancer*? Sounds rather revolutionary, but the answer is almost certainly "yes," because runners almost never smoke. A quick refresher course on the Surgeon General's reports on smoking and health will remind us that smokers suffer considerably more than non-smokers from several forms of cancer, not only lung cancer. Smokers get the lion's share of emphysema and bronchitis. Worse yet, smoking is one of the best-defined risk factors for heart disease. So that among his other duties, today's coach can help set young people on the non-smoking path. No words need be said; no sermons are needed. A delight in vigorous activity carries the non-smoking habit with it.

Constipation is a subject not often considered in relation to physical activity. Vigorous activity, such as running, seems to promote regularity, like the popular high-fiber foods. Runners are seldom constipated, in my experience. If this is true, they probably enjoy relative freedom from hemorrhoids, varicose veins and diverticulosis in later life.

Some confusion has existed about the usual effects of an aerobic exercise program on *blood lipids*. There are two lipids of major interest: cholesterol and triglycerides. Our recent studies have indicated that *triglyceride* levels are remarkably low in groups of male runners aged 30-60, about one-half the level in relatively sedentary men. Women runners were even lower than male runners, and again they showed levels of triglyceride about one half that of sedentary women of the same age. It is generally considered that low triglyceride levels are desirable for heart health. Interestingly, the women runners thus have more *body fat* (as a percent of total body weight) than male runners, but they have lower levels of fat (triglyceride) in the blood. It seems probable that some aspect of fat metabolism in women accounts in part for some remarkable feats of endurance by women in recent years.

Blood *cholesterol* levels in runners (male or female) were found to be somewhat lower than in sedentary controls of the same sex. Recent findings at Stanford have shown that the distribution of this cholesterol among the minute particles that carry lipids in the blood—the lipoproteins—is very favorable in runners. Such favorable patterns are also found in the populations in which heart disease is relatively rare. In other words, the "total cholesterol count" is not the whole story, and again the very active person appears to be blessed with the healthful pattern.

In summary, the coach or physical educator today enjoys a remarkable opportunity to give his charges not only a record-breaking performance in their early twenties, but also an enduring delight in vigorous activity that will help protect them from the ravages of modern diseases for the rest of their lives.

On Nourishment

There are so many different approaches to diet and nutrition that at times you want to throw up your hands and say, "I'll eat whatever I choose." This is not only true for overweight people, but athletes, and people in excellent health. Americans don't have a single national character for food. So we use the opportunity to create an individual food lifestyle using the infusion of all the foods of all the traditions which have entered our country.

I heard a story once about an Italian village that had no record of a heart attack for many years. The people were portly, they didn't exercise, and there were no mineral springs. What did characterize their culture was that they ate and laughed together regularly.

I have been in situations in which a "macrobiotic" friend couldn't eat at festive occasions. The food was too hot, too spicy, not balanced with the other foods. Others were drinking, laughing, and carrying on. A time to be remembered, perhaps. What a drag to miss out on some of the festive occasions of life.

I've seen a few world-class athletes drink and smoke the night before track meets. I've heard some of them insist on common, regular diets, drink cokes, eat "junk foods," and say this was even the proper way to eat for athletics. Frank Shorter, America's foremost distance runner, at a recent talk said sleep was more important than eating.

110

And so it goes with food. At times I can't care less about what I eat, other times I know I can get by on sleep and exercise. But I feel so much lighter and more energetic whenever I pay attention to what I eat. I am going to give you some suggestions for eating. The rationale for proper eating by authorities will vary, but for me, the reason for eating properly is that it feels so much better than eating poorly. There is no worse feeling than exercising and feeling good, clean, wondrous, and then fill yourself up with something that doesn't agree and then end up belching, burping, being constipated, having diarrhea, upset stomach, or just feeling overall flat.

I rely almost exclusively on the two people I respect most in the field of nourishment and food—Percy Cerutty and Win Paris. Win Paris and I met at Catalina Island in the summer of '74 at Percy Cerutty's training camp. Paris originally founded Jack LaLanne's health spas, and was instrumental in beginning numerous nutrition companies. He is now the president of Super-Fitness America.

I'm going to give you some ideas to consider concerning your diet. Think about them and see how they fit into the normal eating patterns you now have. I don't believe you need radical changes in your eating habits. It could only mean substituting a protein drink in the morning, for your "Danish and a cup of coffee," taking a few vitamin supplements. Adhering to some basic do's and don'ts will help your food intake be beneficial to your physical conditioning plan rather than a battle to wage.

- Don't eat or drink unless you are truly hungry or thirsty.
- Eat slowly.
- Don't miss meals.
- Never shop for food when hungry.
- When hungry try having a liquid rather than a meal.
- Eat less bread and make it whole grain.

- Boil, bake or broil instead of frying meat. Fish has more protein than beef and less calories.

- Be aware of the sugar in processed foods like catsup.

- If you omitted one pat of butter daily you could conceivably lose five pounds a year.

- If instead of eating one cup of baked beans you ate a cup of green beans you would save 290 calories.

- Win Paris: "In many cases people are *overfed* and *undernourished*. They eat too much quantity and too few quality foods. These bodies are stuffed and starved at the same time."

I'm not going to give you detailed lists about foods, or tell you how to fix a recipe. You can get that from other sources. What I want you to do is develop your awareness about what you are eating. Read the labels on food products. Processed meats contain preservatives that may be harmful to health. Extremism and cultism is not beneficial to health. As Cerutty said, "Vegetarianism as a humane cult has value. Vegetarianism purely as a dietic cult has not."

- Milk and animal fats should be taken in moderation.

- Rats in a laboratory die quicker eating white flour than nothing.

- Salt in iodized form is harmful to your body. It upsets sodium potassium balance, constricts blood vessels, alters blood pressure. Sea salt or sesame salt are good substitutes if you must have salt.

- Medical researchers have estimated that your body must develop two miles of additional capillaries for every ten pounds of fat you accumulate.

And so awareness is the key to using food for additional vitality. As Cerutty put it:

A philosophy of foods, when the appetite for food is not debased, when the food eaten is plain and wholesome, when the eater realizes the nature and value of various foods, then his enjoyment of simple, plain, and natural foods will be enhanced to an extraordinary degree.

Here are some basic theories of Paris:

- Eat small portions of food slowly.

- Eat fresh foods as close to the natural state as possible.

- Refrain from sugar, preservatives, pesticides, artificial additives, steroids, salt, and fried foods.

- Rest the digestive system one day a week by intaking only freshly squeezed fruit juices.

- Eat in a pleasing relaxed atmosphere.

- Eat foods created by nature, not artificially created by man.

- Chew food thoroughly to promote assimilation and prevent constipation.

- Drink natural liquids from natural sources and spring water.

More to think about:

- Symptoms that your digestive system is having problems are burping, belching, constipation, diarrhea, upset stomach.

- Assimilation is one of the keys to health. Continual eating causes a continual flow of digestive juices. These excess digestive juices such as hydrochloric acid and pepsin, make organs like your pancreas, kidneys, and liver overwork.

- Cerutty: "If you pinch the loose flesh on your abdomen between your thumb and forefinger, and you find you have more than half an inch of fat in that area, consider yourself several pounds overweight."

- It is best to take in fluids at reasonably regular intervals and only two or three times a day.

Cerutty:

- Keep a scale in your home.
- Breakfast is not the most important meal of the day.
- He who overcomes belly-hunger overcomes all.
- Clothed bulk may look impressive; naked bulkiness is repulsive.

So, there are many ways to diet. The good thing about a diet that focuses on drinks, like the popular protein drinks, is that there is a lot of leeway given on the times when you can eat. Feasting and fasting is a way I have found which makes eating more enjoyable than constantly filling up the stomach. There is a man who used to have a pizza shop in Petaluma, California who now serves his pizza at various houses among friends in Mill Valley. His name is Carlo Bambini. His pizza is made with special dough and garnished with imported cheese and olives, pepperoni from Capri, spices from Naples, onions and green peppers from his garden in Petaluma. His pizza is the ultimate feast. Think about it.

Six-Week Training Program Diary

The Commitment

It is a joyous time—starting our training program together. It is the first time in a long while that our family is doing something together that is not work-oriented.

After the running and stretching down at the field, we came home and discussed how we were going to set up a program for ourselves. I felt a little resentment at Bobby for not listening, and I couldn't help but start to think of the ways in which I would help him keep up with the program. Ever since I can remember he has had weight problems. I always worried about it. I have forced him to go on weight reducing programs, but the real problem is his temperament. He has always been a sort of brooding boy. Staying inside during the day, when the other boys were out playing. He did well in school, but his work lacks any enthusiasm. He never has had the exuberance of other youngsters, but it was hard to criticize him because he did so well in school. There was no way to be angry at Robert. One day the boys in his class had made him feel wanted in a neighborhood game, and when he became frustrated, not being able to keep up with the others, they made fun of Robert.

Jill, our daughter, was just the opposite. Her athletic ability seemed to be almost a slap in his face. She was almost 13 now, and had always been a "daddy's girl." Even though I tried hard not to become concerned about her inclination toward physical activity, the "tom boy" way she lived worried me greatly.

Howard and I have been married for 18 years. I am 43

years old, and he is 47. He has been successful as an architect in a respectable firm, but although the dedication he has to his work has paid off in our material well-being, emotionally Howard has died somewhat. He has lost the dreams of his youth, and is becoming content with taking care of his family and security. I can sense that a large part of himself feels his life is over.

We both decided to try a physical fitness program. We thought of joining a local health club, but it seemed one of our friends was always trying to sell their membership because they couldn't find the time to use the facilities. As I am writing this we are embarking on a program which may bring us the satisfaction we are seeking.

Howard and I both began jogging intermittently. It was hard to neglect the jogging fad, as everything you read suggested that jogging was the quickest form of physical conditioning. We had gone through the same routine three or four times, until Howard couldn't get out of bed one day, and then when I drove to the high school track to run could not finish one lap. When some of my friends ran by me while they were talking to each other, I thought I would almost die. Even if jogging were the most tremendous conditioner in the world, it was boring, and I needed something more stimulating. In *Beyond Jogging*, Spino talked about various ways of moving, ways of thinking, and you didn't have to run laps around the field. So we decided to try. We chose days when the family could follow the program together, learning the techniques for relaxation and doing activities for alleviating the boredom.

The first day everything went well. The techniques were easy to follow, and we were not tired out by the training. I guess what we really want from all this is to rediscover the dreams we had about a family. The years have taken us over, and our family unity is only prevalent at Christmas. One day in the future, we want to regain the hope we had when we first came together.

Pre-Assessment 2

The day after tomorrow we will take the pre-test. I am a little concerned for Howard, afraid he will try too hard, and for Robert because I don't want him to become discouraged. Jill has been asking all day what a certain timing might mean. She wants to see what a mile feels like. I just hope I can run a mile! There is a lot of tension building toward this first timing, and I am glad we will have three days before we are tested. The workout on this second day is relatively similar to the first day. I feel somewhat confident now about shuffling, shake-up, fresh swing and tidal breathing. Robert has not been excited but he hasn't complained either. Howard has been excited about having the family together for group readings of the breathing and innerspace sections. I am happy that I can do the workout without other people knowing what I am doing.

Pre-Assessment 3
We had no physical practice today, but we did the usual stretching exercises. Howard read about visualizing, or picturing ourselves in the time trial tomorrow. I have been enjoying the deep sense of relaxation, and what we are now doing is called mental practice. We are practicing in our minds how we are going to run the mile tomorrow.

Time Trial Day
Jill wanted to go first. I knew she would do well, but I was afraid Robert would lose interest if he saw her doing so well and enjoying it. But Robert was enjoying himself in the activity. He didn't say much, but he didn't complain either. There seemed to be an attitude of stick-to-itiveness coming over him. It was amazing to me that we all seemed to be experiencing a change in attitude. When I thought I was a failure when I couldn't run a mile around the track, it became impossible to run a mile around the track, and also it made it impossible to enjoy myself. The three days or preparing we had done to "tone" ourselves for this pre-race assessment had already begun to free me from the fear of facing the track. I felt a strong indication that I would keep up this program. Instead of caring about how I felt or about the time (which was really ridiculous), I focused now on keeping moving as well as I could. So I ran the mile, stopping maybe three times, and finished in 9 minutes and 17 seconds.

Howard chose to run for six minutes rather than a

mile. He felt that would take the competitive edge a bit off of the experience for him. He had been playing tennis a few times a week, so he had some semblance of physical fitness. Still, Howard was right in choosing the six minutes. Even at that I could see the concentration in his brow as he prepared to start. Hopefully the month's program will eliminate a lot of this overachieving. There was a little part of all of us that resisted the imposition of running a test, but we would feel cheated after a month's work at not knowing what our progress was. Howard chose to run the six minutes, but then calculated that he had run about a 7:30 mile pace. I want the program to work for us, and if Howard needs to go through some of these things, perhaps I need to be more tolerant.

Jill said the mile reminded her of testing they do in her gym class. She had been on some junior high school running teams, and her physical ability and temperament seemed just right for athletics. She seemed to enjoy the test, and as the time for her run came closer, you could sense her going inside herself, Jill ran the mile in 5 minutes and 45 seconds. She finished really exhausted, and it took her about ten minutes to recover her sensibility.

Robert was not as shy about facing the timing as I thought he might be. We all made sure that it was the mile rather than the six-minute test which he wanted to do, and he agreed he wanted to run the mile. Now he was standing on the track in his old gym sneakers and a tee shirt on his chubby frame, and I knew there would be no way to stop him from completing the four laps. He went huffing and puffing in what seemed like a year. Sure he stopped once, but he started running again and then there was no stopping him. His time was 8:09, and he finished truly exhausted, gasping for breath and almost crying. I saw Robert that day as I had never seen him before. I was proud of him. Not like a clutching mother; for the first time I really admired him. He smiled at me, and it was a connection long lost, saying his space was his own.

I felt really proud of us, and knew we would keep up with the program. It is just a few minutes out of each day. There was definitely a qualitative searching and looking at self by each other that we had not done in years. I am hopeful.

Day 1
We had a meeting yesterday and decided what schedule we would use for the program. Because there is a tendency for us to get scattered once the day begins, we felt the mornings were the most important time we could spend together. Everyone would get up 30 minutes earlier than usual and we would do the physical parts of the program before breakfast. Lately we had been experimenting anyway with the idea of eliminating big breakfasts for fruit, jam and teas. Just something to warm the body up.

On this day we learned a few new techniques; tidal breathing, surging, power running. We spent the first few minutes of the session going over these new techniques, and then incorporated them into our running. It was really good going to the track, and running on the grass sections of the field. I liked the short intervals because they allowed me to rest in between. For the first time I could be on the field, enjoying other people instead of seeing myself competing with them.

I am trying to do the visualizations, the picturing, in the way the program suggests. I know for sure I am more relaxed. The meditation we are doing is called the "light meditation." After relaxing we picture a light over our heads and in stages draw the light into our bodies. A couple of times I've really gotten away from myself, into a place where I was watching my body and was actually someplace else. The whole thing sort of scared me. It is kind of incredible how quickly we have gotten into the routine of doing these exercises, as if we had been doing them together for years. The strange thing is that in our minds, in our imagination, we have been a family oriented towards this involvement, but we never had a framework that fit, we never had a program that would take us step-by-step. Now we have set time aside, we have measured courses at the high school track and on the road.

Day 4
Tomorrow will be our rest day, but today the bottom dropped out of our training. For three mornings everyone got up bright-eyed and bushy-tailed ready for the training. Last night Howard had an emergency in the

office and didn't get back from an evening meeting until 2
A.M. At least twice a month something like this happens to
Howard, but I had become so insensitive to his schedule
that usually I didn't even notice what time he got in. But
now it was a big thing. Always after these late nights he is a
bit grumpy in the morning and it usually takes him a day
or two to catch up. Robert came down with a cold, and he
said his legs hurt. Instead of the usual morning
enthusiasm during the last five days, there was only Jill
and I. Jill ran off to school saying she would get her run in
on the way to school. I went back to the book to try to get
a hold on what to do in this case. I made a resolve to stick
to the running, and to have the session together tonight
with Howard reading to us from the program. I didn't
want to become aggressive but it was easy to sense the
pitfalls.

At the dinner table everyone was a bit embarrassed.
Robert was down with a cold, but I was going to be a "bad
mother" and let him work out with the cold. It was a light
one and it would only last a few days, but if he didn't
continue with the rest of us it would be a blow to his
personal integrity. I felt like the captain of a ship,
watching out for storms: "Okay mates, we have let off for
shore, there is no going back." We would succeed, I knew
for sure when Howard took us into the living room and we
did a new imagery technique to learn to manipulate the
density of our energy from heaviness to lightness. We
were so happy to be back in our routine, so glad to be rid
of the letdown of each other earlier in the day, the guilt at
missing our higher hopes.

Day 10
The workout this morning went very well. Today we were
on the road, doing our fartlek running. My loop is 2½
miles long. During the workout I did about ten different
intervals measuring my progress along telephone poles.
We all warmed up by shuffling for the first three minutes
and then each went our separate ways. I was a bit
concerned about Robert being out there without the
group support, but he seemed to enjoy it. Howard passed
by some neighbors, and in his new sweat suit he looked
very impressive. Jill did her workout running to school;

she needs the training less than all the rest of us, but I am concerned about her following with us so she remains one of the family.

In the evening we did a body-image meditation in which we look at our body as it presently is, and then imagine—through the use of clouds, hills, and visualized sunshine—a new body. I had the strongest feeling that the reason my body doesn't react often to athletic training is that I want to look good for other people rather than feeling good about myself. If I don't feel good from the inside, I will never make the right transitions. It was a good day with a few very important insights. We all did our stretching together.

The chart is on the kitchen wall, we are becoming a running family.

Day 12

A day of stretching and running at the track. We woke up this morning tired again. But all of us knew how guilty and depressed we felt missing a day last week, so we got in the car and drove to the track. My workout was very hard for me today. I seem to have developed a pain in the front of my legs. The book talks about these being shin splints. Sometimes this happens when you change the surface that you are running on. For me, I think, it is just running all these miles. The stretching helps but this is a hard place to stretch. The whole thing worries me because I was doing so well. The pain does seem to subside when I am on the grass, and starts to go away. I had to cut my workout in half, as was suggested in situations like this. By the end of the day, and in the meditation, I felt much better and the panic had subsided. The meditation of sitting on a rock and visualizing the sun beating on the pain, and then 100s of little fingers massaging, really worked. By the time the day was over I had "figured out" the injury, and I will give myself three or four slightly easier days to make sure it is gone.

Day 18

Today was an easy day with only light stretching and meditation and shuffling and shake-ups. The day after we will have a "repetition run." This is to get ourselves

prepared to put it all together in our final assessment. It is
called "task specific training" and is like a practice race,
only we are only supposed to run 70 percent effort at good
swing. We are all happy today for the easy running and a
little apprehensive. Robert has made such amazing
transitions in these few days. Once or twice he didn't want
to run, and said so. Once he ran away into his books or
some other complaints, but mostly he has stuck with the
new image, and I have been very proud of him. Jill is still
nonchalant. I think she is somewhat embarrassed to be
out there with all of us. She is the top athlete in her class,
and I don't blame her for wanting to be independent.
Howard and I decided that she only has to come when we
run on the track, and that she can do the regular workouts
by herself if she promises to do them all. Howard says he
feels better at work, and that the program is working for
him beyond his hopes. I wish the innerspace techniques
would bring him out of his shell more. I feel he still is not
talking, although a number of times I have seen him in
mental practice or in relaxation really looking like the
man I remember from so many years ago. I am really
happy about it all. The chart still grows on the wall.

Day 20
Today was not like the pre-test on which you almost want
to do poorly so that you can show top improvement at the
end. These are not races and should not be seen as such. In
fact the main plan is to start out slowly and finish as if you
were stepping downward on a gas pedal. According to our
charts we all had different distances to run. We started
with our usual stretching, and did a mental rehearsal
meditation. We laid down on our backs, visualized
ourselves breathing out our fingertips, and pictured a spot
of tranquility inside ourselves, then pictured ourselves
running our distances around the track feeling calm,
relaxed, running smoothly. My distance was one and a
half times around the track, the target time was 2 minutes
and 40 seconds. I felt afraid and awful for the first half of
the lap, and then the momentum of the run took over and
for the first time I can almost ever remember in my life I
felt like an athlete, and was really involved in trying to hit
my time. It may sound silly, but I charged off the last

straightaway and finished the first lap in one minute and 27 seconds. I was as elated as I can ever remember being. It was like being perfect in a dance class. I appreciated the build-up that went into this situation. Howard had to run an 880 and ran what he termed a credible 3 minutes and 30 seconds. Jill matter of factly ran her 660 in 1 minute 58 seconds. Robert really didn't follow directions. He had only to run a 660 in 3 minutes and 45 seconds, but he bombed out and sprinted as hard as he could for the first half of the run and literally finished in a walk in 3 minutes and 56 seconds.

Once I was a child and ran for the joy
   of movement.
I grew older and my body and the image
   of what happiness it could give changed.
I grew much older and all I can think of
   is an elderly lady looking out at a leaf
   falling to the ground wondering
   where my life has gone.
Today I ran once around a running track
   as hard as I could and rather than feeling
   I was dying.
It felt as though I was saving my life.

After 20 days I still feel the changes happening in me. Not only in the track workouts but in the ordinary events of my life. A lot of tension around the house has gone. We have a family outlet, although we often train alone now. I have more pride in myself. When I go to the supermarket I want to see other people. I ran the 660 time assessment with satisfaction.

Day 30

There are days of relief, days of fear, days of soreness, days when I don't want to go out. I have the feeling that I don't really have to go through the entire 42 days. What I have done is enough. It is a sense of stopping when I just am about through the tunnel. I sense that I may stop; I can't tell if I am addicted or not. Yes, some of the workouts have hurt. But as soon as I think they are all going to hurt, an easy one comes along. I am beginning to learn about my own patterns, and the patterns of getting in shape by following the program. I feel myself changing in many subtle ways.

Day 42

I ran the mile today. The final day of the 42-day program. Yes, I improved a whole level. But that was the least of the reward. Somewhere, deep inside of me was a feeling of being strong, really strong for the first time since I can remember. I felt a satisfaction and confidence that I had never believed I would feel. I have lost eight pounds, and am a dress size smaller. The same kind of thing has happened for all my family. We are more together. As our shoes get that worn feeling, I don't think we will ever stop this running thing. Well, maybe not. I don't know right now. I feel like another person. And that other person is a lot lighter in the world.

My Own Voyage

You have changed quite a bit in six weeks; I've been going through it for twenty years. I'm still changing my approach and adding things. There are the basic things— I've learned to live without a coach. If someone wants to time me, that's great, but the stopwatch on my wristwatch gives me independence. I can run for effort without needing the reinforcement of a time, and that is a liberation.

I've learned to chart the state of my own body better. Meditation has helped a lot on this score. In the past I would plow through soreness, fatigue, colds—anything to get in my quota. I'm finally committed to stretching, and I am less sore after hard efforts. I know the range of my movements. I want to be flexible for its own sake. My aim is an East/West body, not a fast time.

I've found that Cerutty was right in saying when you are ready for the right teacher or a new path, it presents itself. As do most runners, I have a tendency to overspecialize—one hundred miles a week and not much variation. I was sore for weeks, suffered from ennui, and had dreams that I was in prison (symbolic of my body, I think). I loved running most of the time, but it got to be a pain being stiff a lot of the time. I had started half a dozen yoga classes, dabbled in Feldenkrais exercises, and had begun many step-by-step stretching manuals. I tried to do the most basic stretching exercises each day. I never did them.

Over the last few years at conferences and workshops, I occasionally bumped into Ken Dychtwald. After a while I would usually complain about my stiff body. We would vow to get together but never did until Ken took the initiative and called me and asked if I would like to be his private student. I am very fond of Ken, he is a combination of a city kid and young intellectual. At twenty-seven, he is already a veteran of the human potential movement. The author of the book *Bodymind*, he directs a center, Sage, for people over sixty-five years of age.

Ken explained to me that it didn't matter how far I could stretch. "It's all an edge," he said. "It is only a line of demarcation. Playing at the boundaries is the most important thing." In addition to the insights he shared with me, he also worked on my weak points. "Most people usually work on the places they can stretch easily, and forget about the weak points." He gave me exercises for my lower back, hamstrings, and pelvis.

The same day I started with Ken I went to Mike Murphy's for a workout. Instead we ended up at a local bar overlooking the ocean harbor. We watched people getting off the ferry, on their way home from work.

I had fallen off the habit of meditating. I would begin and then fall off—not be consistent. That day I pledged to do twenty minutes twice each day, beginning with simple observation of thoughts. Mike's only instruction was to quote the Mother of the Aurobindo ashram, "If you miss one day, you go back three."

After a week I was concentrating on ideas like restlessness, and detachment. Then, counting of breaths, stopping of thoughts. Taking the natural sounds of the world and having them be part of my consciousness. One night my wife Judith and I had a lecture on the "Big Bang" theory of the origins of the universe. "Did you know that the universe is ever-expanding and has no edge?" asked

Murphy. Try that one as a meditation, mixed with the fact that our bodies are not solid—we are a non-solid being living within an ever-expanding universe.

All kinds of information now makes new sense. A. J. Lewis, the chief American researcher on Soviet self-regulation practice, said the great Russian poet Mayakowski would "write poetry while running, tripping over rocks."

When I fight off the need to improve with the notion that I am looking for a whole psycho-physical improvement, I will become the runner I want to be. When I become part of the force of my meditation, operate smoothly from a quiet, powerful source of endless creation, I will grow in my running as well as teaching. My deepest core knows I am getting ready for larger voyages.

The Way of the Warrior—or Will I Become an Extremist?

By this time you may be telling yourself, "I can't follow this kind of schedule—I am not an extremist. I need something just to get me back in shape. You know, a little bit here, a little bit there. So I can wear the bikini I always wanted to wear, or at least get into a size smaller clothes." If I were to tell you it is often easier—I don't mean more enjoyable, or spiritual—to plunge to the top of a sand dune than to jog around your block, you probably wouldn't believe me. But it is true, and it is also true that if you get "stuck" on this new life you won't be able to do without it. You will feel deprived without your daily shot. And if someone says to you, "You look so much better," you will flash inside yourself while they look at appearances.

Sometimes people succeed because they will not let the outward situations of life stop them. A certain willpower, and determination to succeed is necessary. This "steeling of the will" is only a prerequisite for a higher motivation, a yearning for the highest quality of life possible. If you are extreme about taking care of your body, if you wear your sweat clothes around the house in the morning because the morning is a good time for you to work out, if you change your *priorities* so that having a physical workout or a spiritual break is just as important as making a few more dollars, you'll get physical change—and probably the dollars too!

Emil Zatopek was perhaps the greatest distance runner in the modern era. In the 1956 Olympics he won the 5,000 and 10,000 meters and also the marathon. Once when unable to workout because of an injury, he placed his wife (who was an Olympic javelin thrower) on his shoulders and ran in place in his bath tub. He would do anything to continue his training routine.

Percy told me a story about Herb Elliott a day after he lost an 800-meter race. The race had been run on the spur of the moment in the town of Sorrento, near Cerutty's training camp at Portsea. It was one of the few races Herb Elliott ever lost in a career in which he never lost a 1,500-meter or mile race. The day following the defeat, Herb trained so hard on the Portsea property that he was seen hanging on the fence in order to catch his breath. Someone supposed that Herb was no doubt atoning for "giving up" in the race. "Let the bastard die," raved back Percy as he jumped kangaroo-like in response.

I have the desire every so often to destroy myself on a run. Somehow this instinct to fling myself into the world and out of myself must be satisfied. Often I will run up and charge down a sand hill many times. Usually, if I am really into it, beginning a fresh interval up while still gasping for air. At times I have cried afterwards. Somewhere an instinct rises in me that must be satisfied. There is an impulse and desire for change. I want to integrate myself in a new way, kill off the old. I want to be more than I presently am; I'm searching for a new way of acting and being. The intensity that builds inside me is a yearning to kill my old self. From the destroyal comes the new, integrated me. Sometimes after these experiences I need to pray or cry.

Some could say this behavior is slightly abnormal: The impulse for change has merit, but the action comes from masochism and not a sense of delight; true spiritual satisfaction transcends this behavior; this is just the opposite of what one seeks to find in sport, and after I find myself this behavior will not be necessary.

All I can answer to this is that there is a bond between dreamers, friends that share a vision that corresponds to this destroy-and-create process. It is the need for a release after the tension of seeking, or the desire to abandon oneself fully to the activity so you can be free from the volcano within.

Through the years I have sought others in attempts to define and share our destinies: Vision of an athletic yoga—taking the journey deep into the body's access to psychic mystery; the ideal of a brotherhood that defines itself, and keeps each other to the mark; to temper each other's madness, but give it the room to seek the adventures always strewn with dangerous circumstances; becoming a vanguard not by trying, but because the energy seeks release, like the passion that emerges running the sand dune.

If you run the sand dune and feel the cleanness, you can join the journey without interfering static. I am still struggling for running room, my emotions are still my master. The small openings are glorious. One way they come is through release, the spirit that calls me to run the sand dune. As I tell you this I know you will understand and be both fearful and wonder. You will see, but not see. Some of this is your own seeds ungerminated, the language I haven't been able to make sense of, the way of life that feels uncomfortable. I can only say again, "killing" yourself on a sand dune is easier than jogging around the street, and who can tell in what new form you will emerge?

Innerspace

There is a necessity greater than physiological improvement for using your body in an athletic way. This is true
for people seeking optimum health as well as competitive
athletics. Some people use sport as a process whereby they
move towards their true being. They seek to accumulate
experiences that lead to creating a personality. Another
way is to find the source of your character as it now exists.
These aims can be simultaneous and accumulative as you
work towards a state of calm expectancy in which action
and contemplation create a pathway.

The health seeker and the athlete are different, but they
harbor on the same docks. The life reason is the same
whether you jog around the block, do calisthenics in the
bedroom, or run hundreds of laps in an indoor gym. The
health seeker talks about physiological accomplishments
as if they were badges to impress, rather than experiences
to give joy. The competitive athlete often cares so much
for timing, that in a subtle way training is more enjoyable
than racing. The competitive athlete visualizes success as
a wondrous experience, but even in winning, the emotions
expressed aren't what is deep inside. Too often it is the
dilemma of post-performance ennui. The athlete returns
to the house after a championship performance and kicks
the refrigerator. The only satisfaction is a pat from the
coach, and then back to normalcy, back to training which
is the real satisfaction. Spirituality is not brought
forward; it is not even recognized. The body improving on

its way back to being clay. Without spiritual advancement, sadness sets in.

In recent years, millions have attended growth seminars. The release that people experience when they are given the opportunity to relax is enormous. The smallest thrust towards letting go gives excesses of good energy. Often long-held-in emotions are released, the patterned body response gives in to what has for a long time wanted to come to the surface. An internal "code" of personal self-image happens. During this process of awareness, you experience an expansion of self. The growing is not simply accumulative, it is physical growth. To achieve the psychological breakthroughs you have to deal with the effects on the body of the unconscious, in all its forms. Touching on psychodynamic elements is like disturbing a bee hive. The bees come out and you have to deal with them. In getting the honey, you also suffer some stings. So it is with dealing with emotional, psychodynamic issues in a sporting context. Relaxing can be accomplished without probing deep inside the unconscious, or the body can be a gateway into deeper problems that may be lurking in the unconscious.

Physical prowess moves forward in a straight line. You get back what you put in, and you get it back fairly quickly. In this way it is accumulative. You will release energy back into your body through running. Through physical exercise the best forms of bioenergy are made available.

Awareness and Sport

Somewhere among the competitive athlete's fortitude for achievement, the poet's description of wonder, and the mystic's ability for transcendence is a new psycho-physical paradigm, a different way of living. For those of us who grew up attending high school gym classes, went to college football games, and now rush off to health spas, there is no context from which to view our bodies as entities able to blend with our spirit. Running is a somewhat systematic discipline that contains the framework for a yogic practice.

But, if this new fusion of practice is to be authentic, we must be aware of truths discovered in other traditions. In many Indian sects the orientation has been to escape from body into spirit. To them, the physical world is only *maya* (illusion), something to escape from. We must take a larger view and try to bring the spiritual energies developed through our awareness into the physical world, the actual body.

We must come to the understanding that inner dynamics can be spiritual without being religious. I mean religious in the way of thinking of yourself as a Buddhist, Moslem, or Christian. We must approach the unity of mind and body through a practical point of view. Our goal is blending inner self with the moving body. No religious belief system is necessary.

* * *

I practice three ways of using awareness in running. The first is a very simple version of *meditation*—the observation of thoughts, breathing, or inner process where you are able to separate what you are thinking, feeling, or doing with the attitude of an observer or fair witness.

The imagery, or *visualizations*, you carry in your head while running is your stream of consciousness. By getting yourself into a deep state of relaxation and implanting images, ideas, or mental processes into your consciousness, you can use these visualizations for easier, more pleasurable running.

Guided fantasy is a non-moving meditation in which a story line is filled in by ideas that emerge from the participant. Examples of this approach are given throughout this book.

This consciousness exploration will be more subjective than your physical conditioning. If nothing else it will make you more relaxed, and enable you to reach an inner calm that is difficult to achieve in the haste of modern life. This integration of calm with running may form new channels in your consciousness, your personality. You may find new mind/body connections that are new parts of yourself.

This kind of awareness has importance for all of us—from the championship athlete to the person seeking optimum health. Through awareness, there is more enjoyment and a better understanding of the process of athletic achievement.

Inner exploration has brought me meaning. I have a place on the left side of my chest that feels like a tight ball when I meditate. If I sit long enough it will begin to let go. Sometimes my legs feel numb, I can't tell if it is an injury or hypertension. Once while meditating I noticed the source of this tension was in my belly. This spot could be made larger and larger until the numbness began to subside.

This kind of training feels different than physical

training alone. Like "getting hot" in a basketball game, or clicking on a golf course, or getting in the rhythm of an Aikido fall, you may feel a sort of lightness set in, a letting go, a sense of time stopping. You may open your eyes and not want to move for a few minutes. These experiences may cause you to seek the quiet more often. The solitude becomes your conscious home, the place you are what you want to become.

With this kind of training, knowing your body and the integration of mind through running, you are beginning to create a whole new journey. If you are observant, you will notice energy being released into your body while you are running. The energy must be observed with humility, a deference to the powers being unleashed.

The day will come when it all comes together. You are running with a favorite partner, or by yourself. You are dreamy, almost meditating. It is you under the street lamps flying home on a chilled day at dusk—a gold miner coming home over the last hill. At these times, observe, remember, serve the sensations. Let the clear vision of quiet moments lead you to a happy existence with the beauty of the physical world. Seek a calmness that stays and flows like a Japanese tree in a soft wind. Go with the moments. Become through your running, and be transformed from a slave to a seeker.

Intentionality

Consciousness exploration is like any other approach. Sometimes it harvests powerful experiences, other times it's flat. The use of awareness tools in sport is in its infancy. Much experimentation still needs to be done and new possibilities explored and examined. I think it is certain that the future of psycho-physical preparation for both competitive athletes and people of average health will aim at enlarging the scope of the athletic experience.

When talking or thinking about extraordinary occurrences in sport, or the intention of using physical activity as a means to spiritual truths, there is reason to be stymied. Rarely has information of this type been integrated in the overall scheme of a regular athletic practice.

In this context, what does it mean to have an intentional direction? Having an intention means an orientation toward a goal without the certainty of how events will unfurl. You proceed on a commitment separate from empirical fact but grounded in your beliefs. With intention, one waits and works towards realizations, mystically hoping but with the scrutiny of a scientist.

You know pieces of the work are moving towards a synthesis, creating a new form that includes visualizations, running in various styles, and mind over matter techniques. We must all dream, try new things, and live with faithful intentions.

The Way In...

Since the beginning of the Esalen Sports Center in 1973, I have been collecting material on the spiritual aspects of running. In 1966, while running on a road in Syracuse, New York, I had a powerful mystical experience. On that road, something else had taken me, something grand and inexplicable beyond anything I had ever known. When the race was over I seemed to shrink back into my own body. This experience has kept me looking for expanded understanding in running. This experience prompted me to try various forms of mental awareness techniques on myself. It was the framework from which I started blending mind techniques with running methods in the workshops I began teaching for Esalen Institute.

In 1974 I was appointed director of the Esalen Sports Center. This new position stimulated me to do more research and study more experimental approaches to running and sports. As a workshop leader I have tried dozens of techniques, and somewhat like a vaudevillian polishing each aspect of a performance, I have come up with a series of approaches which seem to work.

Ever since 1974, when Percy Cerutty and I did a workshop together at the University of California at Santa Barbara, I have been convinced that my contribution to running would be significant in the areas of psychic and mystical approaches. More recently, I have been working with A. J. Lewis, the leading researcher on psychic self-regulation (PSR). His studies of Russian preparation for the Olympic Games with awareness techniques adds scientific validity to the religiosity of the Indian and Tibetan disciplines.

It is difficult to be complete about a theory for awareness in running. This new approach to sport is in its infancy. In my work I feel as though I am only a beginning meditation teacher. The area is so vast that the pioneer can make a significant contribution to what is becoming a whole new area of sport training and psychology.

Some techniques, such as chanting and visualization, can be done while running. A lot is done separately from the actual movement. With this expanded direction to the teaching of running, we hope to contribute greater meanings.

Competition is not our main motive, though relaxation techniques, guided imagery, and mental rehearsals can enhance performance. There is the hope that the values of winning can be subsumed by personal qualities such as integrity, selflessness, and surrender. Rather than forceful training, the goals may then be sincerity and patience.

The object of this inner exploration is to enhance the pleasure and perhaps the performance of a particular run. The mind uses these images as a series of snapshots, the mental pictures come and go. It is not like a light bulb constantly available to the senses. The preparations are varied. Sometimes we sit in quiet meditation watching thoughts or breaths; other visualizations are introduced just before a particular run (such as seeing a hand behind you pushing you up the field), intricate images or fantasy-like body density, body image changes, surrendering, or disassociation are presented in a story line.

It is interesting to explore the possibility of using the mind as a tool for greater physical performance. Among the most adventurous stories of the uses of consciousness in running is reported in the legends of the *lung-gom* walkers of Tibet who have been known to cover great distances at incredible speeds.

In Lama Anagarika Govinda's *The Way of the White Clouds*, he writes:

> The deeper meaning of lung-gom is that matter can be mastered by the mind. This is illustrated by the fact that the preparatory exercises are mainly spiritual, i.e. consisting in strict seclusion and mental concentration upon certain elementary forces and their visualized symbols, accompanied by the recitation of mantras, through which certain psychic centres of the body, which are related to those forces by their natural functions, are awakened and activated. *Lung* signifies both the elementary state of 'air,' as well as the subtle vital energy or psychic force. *Gom* means meditation, contemplation, concentration of mind and soul upon a certain subject as well as the gradual emptying of the mind of all subject-object relationships, until a complete identification of subject and object has taken place.
>
> In terms of visualization, beginners in the art of the lung-gom are often advised to fix their minds not only on a mentally visualized object—namely the aim towards which they want to move—but to keep their eyes fixed on a particular star, which in some cases seems to produce a hypnotic effect. It is the non-interference of normal consciousness which ensures the immunity of the trance walker and the instinctive sureness of his movements. There is no greater danger than the sudden awakening to normal consciousness. It is for this reason that the lung-gom walker must avoid speaking or looking about, because the slightest distraction would result in breaking the trance.

The lung-gom is only a mystery to me, but there are some techniques I have found useful for shifting concentration. One of these is the use of "soft eyes." This practice is used in the martial arts as a means of making the world seem more mystical. With "soft eyes" (half closed), the world takes on a softer hue, objects don't seem to have definite edges. If you have a visualization in your mind, and use "soft eyes," you can look in and out at the same time.

I have used mental picturing to allow someone to run further than they had suspected they could. They couldn't picture themselves running successfully around the track. Try as they may, after one lap they get discouraged, can't face another step. It is often successful to have people "rehearse" running successfully in their minds. When the anxiety of pain or the humiliation of not finishing comes to the conscious surface, it can then be dealt with.

The enemy of all this is skepticism. It is easy to give up after the first experiments and go back to jogging instead of experimenting with thought, breath, and the power of your mind. What I am proposing is an open imagination. Dreaming and believing bring on unbelievable results. You needn't make any proclamations. You are an experiment of one—keep it that way. Change may happen very quickly, you may even miss the first occurrence.

These are new dimensions of the running experience. There are no charts to guide the exploration. We have many abilities untapped, and archetypes, memories, and dormant energies stored unconsciously. The keys to these doorways in athletics are part of the future.

The Process of the Perfect Runner

There is a connection between what a person feels inside one's self and running with a spiritual intent. My premise is that the body is a tool for transcendence, and that elevating experiences will bring both happiness and faster times.

The goal is to build up a momentum through meditation practices. We want to gear into a realm of consciousness that can then be, hopefully and sometimes spontaneously, transferred to actual running. The process of combining innerspace and running is aided by going to a retreat location. In retreat we can get to know our present states; the creative plane doesn't change, we just become more aware of it. My teacher, Percy Cerutty, often said there is no hurry on the creative plane—there are digits of predetermined destiny. It is this sense of momentum on the path we are traveling which will help us visualize how we can do something beautifully. The beauty is already in us. Just as we sometimes have a sense of meeting someone whom we were meant to come across, or even a setback or challenge that seemed in our life plan, we are now going to sense what we would be like as a perfect runner. The easiest way is to know the state of perfection is already there and the techniques such as autogenic training, mental rehearsal, and biofeedback are only means to discovery. The process of finding your inner perfect runner comes about by slowing down the mental processes that occur simultaneously with the actual running.

The technique I presently use is to attempt to enter a dreamy space by closing my eyes completely to sense my movement, and then begin opening and closing my eyes so that I might get to a point where I am actually inside my body and mind, while being able to see where I am running.

The meditation process begins by lying down with your arms stretched outward. Visualize yourself breathing out through your fingertips while taking deep breaths into the abdomen. After relaxation is achieved, visualize a halo over your head and draw light from it into your body in stages. Picture yourself drawing light first into the bottom of your neck, then into the chest, and finally into the abdomen. This induction is our main means of arriving at a slowed-down state of awareness. After you have done this part of the exercise for a while, follow the light going into the body and concentrate on the place at which you feel the most sensation, power, or energy (whatever your favorite term is), and visualize a large circle in your head, chest or abdomen. Begin breathing into this circle and picture the circle becoming larger or smaller. Let the focus of your consciousness on this circle be your total body awareness. Relate as much as possible to the circle expansion and contraction.

After a few moments of experiencing this sense, stand and begin shuffling slowly around the field. Shuffle with eyes slightly closed so you can stay inside your consciousness. If the sense of the hole you are visualizing disappears, return to a lying position and recapture the picture. At times you will be running and at other times reclined in a meditative position. Moving at the edge of physical performance coupled with internal relaxation and a sense of inner balance has the possibility of harvesting both a spiritual and physical running experience. Allow this innerspace to remain calm whatever the external stimuli might be. In other words, you could be running hard while maintaining inside a kernel that stays calm and soft. As mastery of the inner calm comes more easily, you could add a visualization of yourself running around the field with perfect form and inner calmness. What can happen in these kinds of exercises is that the mental "interferences" that limit our physical potentials can be minimized. Also by talking in these terms and probing the possibilities of linking body, spirit, and mind, an *intentionality* is set in place. The intention to transform running into a spiritual experience can create a conglomeration of events and insights that are by-products of the physical experience. I am often pleasantly surprised that in a group of only semi-active adults, mental preparations such as this sometimes enable individuals who had previously run only three miles in a day to cover six or seven miles. This is done by creating a momentum that limits otherwise negative self-images.

The theoretical question that emanates from these kinds of experiments is: Where do the limits of induced awareness end and physical capabilities emerge? And, is it possible to cut into the soul of the runner, to transcend the psychodynamic and intrapsychic bonds, and by freeing the spirit make physical activity easier and more enjoyable? Perhaps to fathom the deepest natural tendencies will be to make running a gateway into "super being."

If the inner journey is to become a tool for improved enjoyment and performance, the traditional notions of winning and competition will need to be altered. Touching on high spaces, a sense of touching on the threshold of the collective unconscious will all be part of the athletic experience. The process of becoming the perfect runner is only a beginning into this realm. It is all speculative; I know, though, that these kinds of events and energies actually have been unleashed in the athletic arena.

When Percy Cerutty took Herb Elliott aside before his record-smashing run at the 1960 Olympics in Rome, he told him to be guided by his instincts as to when to leap on the pack. Elliott ran like no one else before him had, demolishing the Olympic field and expressing himself in a fuller way than most remember. (Elliott was just chosen by *Track and Field News* as history's greatest all-time miler.) Could it be that he was deep into the wisdom we speak of here? His mastery of pain through imaging is similar to visualizations I present. He would arrive at a state of extreme exhaustion and instead of running the last quarter-mile, he would visualize it in his head, "See a 55-second last quarter in your head." He created his own reality apart and beyond pain and physical limitations.

The concept of the perfect runner is only a means to unleashing energy, a technique to enable a person to touch on their own personal energy, to begin freeing the soul to merge with physical awareness. By developing the whole self we do the body a favor. We have the possibility of becoming angels rather than brutes. In short, we can begin to open the doorways to new paradigms where body meets spirit.

Psychodynamic Possibilities in the Running Experience

People usually don't work with me to receive psychological benefits. I am a coach not a therapist. Sometimes, though, when the body is stimulated, emotional blocks and painful remembrances can be worked with. For this reason, especially in my workshops, I find it helpful to probe the underworld of interpersonal communications before moving into running techniques. After these blockages are worked out, we can move into the physical and spiritual domains.

On occasion I co-lead a workshop with a therapist. This synthesis changes the priority of the workshop. In a group that seeks a larger scope, a psycho-physical potential, the focus is on overall development. By beginning with the interpersonal, there is the possibility for more enjoyable running. It can also allow openings for pathways into theoretical considerations, and allow openings for transpersonal experiences and communications. A colleague, Ozzie Gontang, works with psychiatrist Dr. Thad Kostrubala, author of *The Joy of Running*. Their work as running therapists has revealed many situations in which clients get in touch with archetypal understandings after an hour or so of shuffling. They have found, especially within the framework of the Jungian psychology, running is a passageway into a space from which therapeutic work can be done.

The guided fantasy I use for psycho-dynamic purposes

is a time regression process. It often clears out old concepts, used up images that may be causing tension within the running body. Mom and Dad can go through this process by reading the fantasy below to each other and then discussing the outcomes. This exercise may not be appropriate for children, because it goes back into your childhood. But if you suspect some trauma may have occurred to your children, you might try this with them at an earlier time period than I am suggesting.

Go into a deep state of relaxation by breathing deeply into your abdomen, and relaxing on the exhale. Use one of the standard forms of meditation sitting. As we have done in other exercises, let the breathing progress from your abdomen into your chest and then into your facial area. On each exhale let yourself sink further into the floor or chair on which you may be sitting.

We are going to take a trip back into your past. Actually picture the years flowing by, by visualizing the pages falling off a calendar—1974, '72, '70, '68, '55, and backward, all the way to your first remembrances of physical exercise as a young person. Make the remembrance somewhere from age four to eight or nine. If the experience was a positive, successful one amplify the memory and in your mind see yourself performing and enjoying it with even more kinesthetic delight and pleasure. Make it all richer and more expansive.

If the remembrance caused you pain, frustration, or sorrow, relive the negative event in your memory. Actually remember and bring to the surface the pain of the situation. Notice the place, the clothes you wore, the other children involved if it is pertinent. Try to get to the source of your fear, frustration. Was the pain physical or emotional? Run the event in your mind a few more times. Now you can change that event in your history, perhaps forever. There is no need to carry the memory of it forever. What is done is over!

Free yourself by picturing the event in your mind as you would have liked it to have occurred. See yourself handling the situation well, foreclosing on the problem. See yourself moving with grace, pleasure, and precision.

Let this same visualization be done for a remembrance in your teenage years. Finish by picturing in your mind a successful and pleasurable physical experience that you would like to have in your present daily life.

After this association between past and present is completed, share your process with each other. I have had people being forced to wear and practice in tight ballet shoes, the conflict of father and son over football accomplishment. One woman realized that since youth she had eaten out of hostility. She had dieted only to please others. When she lost weight because of how *she felt*, the pounds gradually melted off. Now she has lost twenty pounds and runs in "fun runs" up to 10 miles.

It is often useful to observe the psycho-dynamics involved in running. Go over to a popular running site to watch. Don't look for speed, although smoothness and aesthetic beauty may come into play. Watch more for the need of people to pass each other, those who seem to be holding back, those who continue to run after the group they have been running with has finished, those who can't run in a group. Watch as a therapist might through a two-way mirror. So many factors can lead to the tight, struggling runner. Dr. Nidiffer, author of *The Inner Athlete*, points out, "By being able to maintain attention on a single thought or feeling a runner can develop a rhythm that will help increase both endurance and pain tolerance."

I have done week-long workshops in which people who have little or no running experience can cover 6 to 8 miles, staying close to their internal processes and using fitness techniques outlined in this book. Running is not just a physical process. Your mind and spirit can't help but be partners over the miles you run.

Moving from Finding Center to Visualizing for Easier Running

The Chinese teach that a person moves and lives in harmony when his awareness is located just below the belly. It is said there is a power and presence that occurs when your sense of self has a grounding, firmly near the center of gravity.

On the other hand, we as Westerners have a tendency to see the world through our intellect. Everything is done within the calculations of the mind. Consequently, we do not move with purpose and intent. Our physical self is at odds with our consciousness, and the resulting action is disjointed.

When we are relaxed, we produce brain-wave frequencies that are conducive toward creative action and thought. These brain-wave frequencies are broken into three categories: theta, alpha, and beta. Theta is the slowest cycle, which occurs while we are sleeping. Alpha is the mid-frequency, produced in meditation and creative thought. Beta is for computation and analysis.

In the centering process you are about to do, the object will be to relax into an alpha state and then move with body awareness to your center of gravity, just below the belly. Our Western habit of cognitive thought often forces our sense of self behind the eyes. With that body orientation we are apt to produce beta-wave frequencies rather than alpha frequencies, which are slower and more creative signals. By moving your consciousness down to the center of gravity, you get into an awareness that enables more relaxed and physically integrated movement.

We will begin by centering ourselves. Start by closing your eyes, and visualizing your personal awareness moving down your body. Your first sense of self may be in your head. It will take time to move towards a more central location. When your awareness seems to become focused near your mid-body, begin walking slowly, and continue as long as your consciousness continues to flow from this area of your body.

Next, choose a partner. Place one hand on their upper chest, and as the partner begins walking with awareness at mid-body, periodically (at uneven intervals) apply resistance to his or her forward movement. The walker should concentrate on steady movement with their focus ahead, moving from center, not anticipating resistance. The spirit of the resistance should be similar to the idea of attacker and attackee in Aikido, a Japanese martial art. The belief in Aikido is that the resistance offered by the aggressor is not competition as we think of it in Western sport, but a kind of gift that opens one to greater potentials. This attitude makes the resistance a helpful feedback, rather than a means of deceivement. The process should be continued until each partner has gotten the "feel" of moving from mid-body. This means you will be traveling back and forth up and down a field, finding center, and giving resistance.

Once this place of awareness is located and you are able to hold it for a period of time, you can use it to run with less effort by combining centered awareness with visualization. By visualization I am referring to the process of creating a picture in your mind to carry while running. Some people visualize easier than others. For some, thinking in pictures is like a series of snapshots. One flash leads to another, and before long an image is being carried fairly consistently. Of course, this picture comes and goes. Because people vary in their ability to visualize, there are a variety of pictures you can use after you are centered. A visualization to integrate with your centered feeling is as follows:

Pinpoint a set of trees or the goal post of a football field about 100 yards away. Picture in your mind a wire stretched between you and this point. Further picture that sitting to one side of the trees or on the goal line is a man with a crank in his hand. He turns a rope that pulls from a harness you can visualize being connected to your abdomen.

You are now standing facing up a field. Go over the visualization once more before you prepare to move. A rope across a span, a person in a tree turning a crank, a rope pulling from your abdomen area where a harness is located. In order to maintain the inner image and still be able to run, open your eyes just slightly, so that you can see where you are going, but try to keep your awareness focused inward. This is called "soft eyes." The rope begins to pull taut, but your legs are anchored in the ground. Sway the pelvis forward, feeling the full tautness of the rope, but still anchored in the ground. You are not ready to be released yet. When the time is correct, give in to the pull of the rope, and allow yourself to be swept up the field.

A similar but somewhat simpler visualization is to locate a pole, tree, or visual object a bit up the field or road. Picture in your mind throwing a rope out to this object and hooking around and letting the rope pull you towards it. This should also be done with "soft eyes."

Concentration

Many times we are faced with a situation in which practice does not make perfect. It is not always the muscles and sinew that enable a person to complete a situation successfully. The deeper execution of the act lies in a place of self-belief and self-confidence.

Lee Pulos, a sports hypnotist, told me about Jackie Stewart, the race-car driver. Stewart had himself programmed so that in the case of a serious mishap he could turn off the ignition, take off his seat belt, open the door, and jump out—all in about 1.5 seconds. He had mentally rehearsed the action in his mind. When the danger presented itself, he plugged into what he already knew and reacted automatically. Watching Dwight Stones, world record high jumper, perform is a similar experience. Oblivious to the crowd he is a tranquil being with a passive demeanor. Other times he is a social bubbly person.

These athletes are using a special way of seeing. They are visualizing themselves as coping effectively with a situation, being relaxed and allowing successive thought patterns to flow through their consciousness.

Sometimes this form of relaxation and concentration takes the form of "settling into an experience." I am reminded of an occasion before the 1976 Bay-to-Breakers cross-city run in San Francisco. It was a typical scene— loud talking, long lines at the bathrooms, anxious looks, people dressed in tuxedos, a wide assortment of costumes.

Eight thousand people had entered the event. The starting line would be three blocks long.

When your mind is scattered, free flowing anxiety takes over. Therefore, if I could relax, not only might I do better, but I might enjoy rather than abhor the actual event.

I was seated on the floor, waiting. My pal Mike Murphy sat beside me. "Let's close our eyes and take in their energy," Mike said to me. Closing my eyes I felt my legs shake. In a few moments I was enjoying the quiet. After a few more moments I felt relieved. I ran 45th place at a 5:09-mile pace.

Here is a meditation I developed for Janet Coles, a young professional woman golfer who was having problems concentrating. The object of this is to visualize yourself successfully completing each step of an act, one step at a time.

Take a relaxed position, either lying on the ground with your palms upward, or sitting in a chair. Begin taking deep breaths into your abdomen. Each time you breathe out, let your whole body relax into the chair or floor. Begin letting go a bit on each exhalation. Go to a deeper level of relaxation each time you breathe out. Next, picture an hourglass in your mind. Remember, pictures like this visualization develop in spurts, little snapshot-type photos that come to mind. You have to connect the lines between the emerging images.

To slow down your breath and calm your emotions, watch your breath as you exhale. While you are watch-ing your breath, visualize the grains of sand falling from the top to the bottom of the hourglass. Remember, only one grain of sand can pass through the hourglass at a time. For example, hitting a golf ball, stay in the moment with your breath, and watch the grains of sand fall as you connect with the ball.

While you are practicing—now that you have made a connection between your breath and the image in your mind—allow a situation that causes you anxiety to come to the surface. See it in your mind, with relaxed one-grain-at-a-time visualization, and complete the situation successfully.

I can't promise this picturing will get you lower scores or faster running times, but it will get you more fully into the experience—which is the real reason for playing, anyway.

Beyond the Physical Limits

A primary focus of the mind/body approach to running is the mastery of techniques for deepening individual awareness. Combining meditation, visualization, and guided imagery deepens your inner contact while sitting or moving. These processes, when combined with a physical training routine, open pathways for the simultaneous experience of the physical, mental, emotional, and spiritual dimensions within yourself. Through this unified approach to the athletic experience, I believe the greater potential of the human being will emerge.

Specific types of mental practice include "witness" meditation to develop a sense of detached observation or "witness" of one's thought forms; energy awareness to become familiar with sensations within the body and explore their relationship to one's physicality; visualization to create a mental image which supports one's physical endeavors; and guided imagery to allow the creative imagination to directly influence one's body. Through experimentation with these and other practices, I have developed specific routines for runners.

Meditation to Create an Altered State of Consciousness While Running

The object of this exercise is to move from sitting meditation to running, maintaining the contemplative state of awareness. Using breathing techniques and guided imagery, a state of consciousness can be created which opens the doorway to greater physical achievement.

To begin, sit in a standard Zen sitting posture, placing your hands in your lap, the left hand in the right palm, with your fingers slightly curled and thumbs touching gently. This may be done in a straight-backed chair with feet flat on the floor or in a seated position on the floor. Eyes are closed. The leader will then begin to guide the meditation. (Continue this breathing for about two minutes.)

Let us begin with an awareness of our breath, breathing into the lower abdomen. Gently guide the air into your lower belly region...Do not force the breathing rhythm ...Allow it to proceed naturally...Exhale slowly and relax...Again, inhale deeply into your abdomen, completely filling the cavity...As you exhale, observe the tensions being released ...Allow yourself to let go

and relax...(Continue this breathing for about two minutes.)

Now breathe only into your upper lungs or chest area...Completely fill the upper chest...Exhale slowly and relax...Continue this breathing pattern, filling the entire chest cavity...Exhale slowly and relax...Inhale and exhale completely and rhythmically...Guide your breath...Observe your body ...(Continue the breathing for about two minutes.)

On the next inhale, fill your abdomen first and then your chest...Observe the incoming breath...On the exhale, release the air from the chest and then from the abdomen ...Each complete exhale brings an ever-deeper calmness and relaxation to your body...Inhale, first filling your abdomen, then your chest...Exhale from the chest and then the abdomen...and relax...Inhale...Exhale... and relax...Maintaining this state of awareness, begin to breathe normally once again....

Continuing your normal breathing pattern, begin to visualize a light about the size of a halo directly over your head...On an inhale, draw light from this halo into your body...First let this light fill your head and spread down to

the bottom of the neck, relaxing each section of your face as the image of light passes through it...Allow your entire neck and head to shine with this light...and relax...

On an inhale, draw the light further down into your body until it fills your chest area...Feel the warmth and nourishment as you continue to relax...Draw the light down further, into your abdomen...See the light completely encompass your breathing apparatus...Visualize this light relaxing and calming your head, neck, chest, and abdomen...(Continue for three to five minutes.)

Now allow the light to slowly recede from your body ...leaving a warm and pleasant glow throughout...As it leaves your head, see the halo slowly fade from sight...and know that it continues to exist as a personal energy source...

You are now prepared to pass into a freer form of inward looking...Let us begin to expand our capacities for self-observation...Begin to observe your thoughts as they pass before you...Open your contact with your "witness self"...Allow whatever enters your mind to pass through your consciousness...Observe it and let it go...You may find yourself immersed in a thought or idea...Observe this process and let it go...Empty your inner mind...Allow thoughts to pass through while the "witness" watches and remains detached...(Continue in silence for 10-15 minutes.)

At this point the group is in a very receptive state of consciousness and should be slowly introduced to movement. This is done with a method which originated from southern Buddhist practice and is referred to as a "Zen walk." At a meditation retreat, called a *zendo*, this meditative walking is often done at intervals between formal "sitting." Traditionally, forty minutes of sitting is followed by ten minutes of "walking." This routine can last for hours or months. The object is to carry the contemplative state of awareness into movement.

The group should stand slowly and form a circle with everyone facing in the same direction to follow a circular path. The leader continues the instruction:

We will begin to carry the meditation into action with a slow walk around the circle...The goal is simply to move with the "witness self" ...Make a fist with your left hand, place it over your navel and cup your right palm over your fist...With eyes gently open, place your left foot forward, allowing your heel to touch the ground first...Gradually shift your weight onto the entire foot ...Hold...Swing the right leg forward slowly and with conscious observation ...Make contact with the heel and slowly rock forward to the toes...Continue this sequence of swing... heel...toe...swing...heel ...toe...slowly and with a deepening "witness" . . . (Continue for three to ten minutes.)

Stop and slowly turn to face the center of the circle. Drop your arms to your sides and allow your eyes to focus softly on a point in front of you . . . Breathe into the spot...Form a relationship between your conscious breath and your object of concentration . . . Observe your thoughts . . . Deepen your inner sense of "being" ...(Maintain for one to two minutes.)

After this process of sitting, walking, and standing, the group is ready for running. The leader continues:

Let us come together and picture ourselves as a primordial band of people...We will begin shuffling at a very slow pace which I will set...Please refrain from talking during this experience...

At this point, a silent group run is begun with attention paid to maintaining a state of concentrated awareness. Someone should be designated to take up the rear so that no one falls way behind the pack. The pace should be determined by the slowest runner in the group. The run can continue for any distance desirable with optional brief stops for meditation. I have led people through this process and continued running up to 8 miles. Some of these people had only run 6 to 8 miles per week previously.

After the run is completed, a short exercise helps bring the group back to an ordinary state of consciousness. The group lies down on their backs and breathes again into the abdomen and out the fingertips. Continue this for about three minutes. It is always valuable to have a short sharing session to end the experience.

Meditation: Lighter and Heavier

The object of this guided fantasy is the manipulation of one's sense of body density. The induction of this exercise is best done with the participants lying on the floor. The leader guides the experience in this way:

> Let us begin this session by focusing on our breath...Breathe deeply into your abdomen...Exhale all the breath and relax...Inhale deeply into the abdomen...And begin to visualize the exhale traveling down your arms and out of your fingertips...Breathe deeply into your abdomen...See the breath leaving through your fingertips...And relax...(Continue for two to three minutes.)
>
> With the next inhale, place your consciousness in the back of your neck...Allow your breathing pattern to continue normally, keeping your consciousness in the back of your neck...With the next inhale, move your consciousness into the small of your back...Experience the small of your back as it contacts the floor...Examine

the world from that perspective...Now begin to scan your body presence, locating any places of tension...Breathe into any place of tension...Allow them to relax...(Allow one to two minutes for scanning.)

Picture a body, a presence other than your physical body, and place this image a few inches outside yourself...We will call this other being your ethereal body...Mentally trace this other being to sense its diameters...Visualize this ethereal body as a balloon and connect it to your abdomen with a string...Poke it with a mental fingertip to create a little more space between the two of you...It will not go too far away because it is secured by the string from your abdomen...On every exhale, visualize yourself filling this presence with a substance lighter than air such as helium...Continue filling on the outbreath until the ethereal body is full and free-floating above you...(So much of life is holding on. Even when there is the desire for relaxation, our physical body does not know how to produce it. The image of the floating cloud places the mentality of lightness outside of yourself and as you give in to the floaty feeling, you actually merge with the deepest parts of yourself.)

Begin drawing this inflated and lighter-than-air presence back toward your physical body by pulling in the connecting string...With each inhale, pull the presence a little closer...Inhale and draw the presence closer until it is just outside of you...Take a big gulp of air and draw the lightness deep inside your physical body...Feel the lightness as a part of yourself, sensing an internal airiness much like a bird must feel...Bask in this lightness and feel your body just barely touching the floor...It is only your will which keeps you from floating away.

At this point in the fantasy the participants may be led into a running experience with instructions to arise while maintaining the feeling of elevation and lightness. Instruct the runners to run *only* while the sense of lightness is clearly present. If it loses clarity, the participant should walk or stop completely and meditate until it returns. Continuing in this fashion often allows a runner to move with an easier stride and less exertion.

An alternative to the running is a continuation of the guided imagery into an experience of heaviness and cleansing. The leader continues with instructions.

Now imagine a valve in your side... Open this valve and let the light airiness escape... Continue until you sense your body lying flat, totally deflated of all internal presence... Imagine yourself devoid of internal substance... An entity without much density, lying on the floor... (Allow two to three minutes for the experience.)

Begin to visualize yourself filling up with a heavy, clean oil... Beginning with the places where your body contacts the floor, see yourself slowly filling up with this heavy substance... Continue until you are sensing yourself as a dense, heavy presence...

Again open the valve on your side and let the heaviness leave your body... Feel the relief of this experience... As the oil leaves your body, it dissolves the pain, anxiety, and self-recriminations you have built up inside... You can see all of these traits becoming smaller and smaller particles, eventually dissolving completely in the oil and disappearing out of the valve in your side... Let the emotional heaviness that you have accumulated blend with the oil substance and allow yourself a released cleansing....

You may feel an emptiness now that you have not experienced before... Again open your valve and begin filling your body with the lighter-than-air substance... On the inhale draw in the helium or spun cotton... As you become full, go into your feeling of being, of presence, of awareness, and experience what it is like to feel internally light and airy... Keep this with you as a place of cleanliness and security... Feel the purity of moment... Now begin to return to your ordinary sense of reality by taking deep breaths into your abdomen and visualize yourself breathing out through your fingertips... As you gradually come back to normal consciousness, slowly open your eyes... Remember your sense of internal lightness where the being dwells in purity... Carry this feeling into this day's physical activity...

Add a Visualization to an Interval

When a group is preparing for an interval run, one of two images is often helpful as a support mechanism. Instruct the group to stand quietly and build a mental picture of a giant hand, as large as a person's back, gently pressing each body forward. Continue this image during the training session. If anyone has trouble with the hand image, suggest an image of a skyhook descending from the heavens, attaching itself gently to the body and pulling it along.

Moving with the Inner Body

This exercise was first introduced to us during a session with Robert Nadeau, the Aikido master. It is aimed at deepening one's understanding of the inner body and allowing this inner sense to guide the physical expression of erupting energy. It is an excellent ritual to do just before training or in preparation for a race.

While in a standing position, allow your attention to be drawn inward and focus on the first two physical locations which come to mind. With eyes closed, breathe slowly and evenly, allowing your concentration to fill these body parts. When you have attained a rapport with these locations, open your mind to any images which flow through. Allow the first image to possess your body and your body to become the image. Allow the second image to carry your body into motion as you express the inner energy in spontaneous form and movement.

In a demonstration of this technique, Nadeau chose the lungs and the small of his back for concentration. As he allowed the images to direct his body, he visualized two rods which raised his arms straight up and lifted him toward the ceiling. At the same time, he felt a stream of water take his body in its downstream current, propelling him forward. He subsequently experienced a release of energy from his upper torso which allowed a greater breadth of physical mobility.

Energize a Partner

Stand facing a partner, arms partially stretched in front of you with your forearms parallel to the ground. Place one palm upward and one palm downward. Your partner stands in a similar fashion with hands positioned one inch above and below yours. Let your eyes remain slightly open without looking directly into your partner's eyes. Begin rotating your hands over each other's in a circular manner. You will begin to feel heat or a tingling of energy. Experience this sensation and allow your mutual energy fields to blend with each other. Drop your hands to your side while you continue to feel the energy you have created together. Turn your back to your partner while he or she begins to gather the energy into a visualized "energy ball." Your partner now places this "energy ball" into the small of your back and spreads it gently and evenly throughout your body. When you feel or sense the transfer of energy, run down the field about 100 yards and either tidal breathe or surge the last half of the interval. Return to your partner and give him or her the same experience.

The techniques described above have been synthesized from various schools of yoga, meditation, the Oriental martial arts, gestalt therapy and other self-awareness disciplines. They have proven to be worthy additions to the training regimens for the variety of runners with whom I work. To add to the repertoire of mental practices, it is good to draw from contemporary research in such areas as medicine and biofeedback.

In recent years, biofeedback research has demonstrated that individuals can learn to control various physiological functions through appropriate visual or auditory feedback from monitoring instruments. Relief from pain, warming or cooling of parts of the body, control of blood flow, and muscular relaxation can be quickly mastered through biofeedback training. All of these internal processes influence a runner's performance and their purposeful direction could expand one's running skills. In addition, I recently learned of the first successful attempt to willfully manipulate the blood-sugar level in a person's body. We wonder just how far this directed self-regulation can go. Will there be a day when the conscious runner directs his or her physiology through an inner guidance system to maximize performance? I think so.

In contrast to the increasing interest in drug-induced physical development, I encourage the application of mental techniques to support and expand physical capacities. The joining of spirit and mind with the body in mutually supportive roles is an emerging frontier gradually capturing our imaginations. Taking a long view, I believe, an appropriate balance of mental and physical discipline will outdistance the drug-reinforced musculatures being cultivated around the world. Running with the inner self is an adventure unparalleled in sport. It is there for all to experience.

The Stillness Within—
Center of Light Visualization

The object of this moving meditation is to develop a quiet source of strength inside that is oblivious to stimulus. You can do this mental exercise as part of your fartlek training. Instead of walking or shuffling as your rest period, occasionally add this workout to your training.

Begin this exercise by lying down on your back and drawing light into your abdomen. On each exhale, let yourself "settle" into the floor. After a few breaths, extend the awareness into your chest, and then into your facial area. Continue by visualizing a white light about the size of a halo over your head.

Throughout the meditation, this light will be useful for focusing awareness and vibrancy. It can be useful for making running easier and more enjoyable. In the first breaths, light is drawn from the halo over your head just down to the bottom of your neck. Focusing awareness on just the head area will tend to relax the face, perhaps right in the act of running. Next draw the light and the energy you bring with it to your chest. Continue by drawing deep into the abdomen and pelvis. As the flow in and out becomes more fluid, use the interval breathing to release tension.

Now that breath and visualized light are inside your body, we will be able to pinpoint a place from which to create stillness. To find your place of vibrancy, draw the light from over your head throughout your body: face, chest, abdomen. Watch your body, emotions, and senses.

You may feel a bit of shock or a stirring of emotion on the

passing of light through the most energetic of these three areas. If you feel absolutely nothing, pretend you do. This sometimes opens up visualizations.

In the area of your choice, visualize a large circle. Locate the perimeter of this circle. Let the circle expand and contract so that it can be a dot or a wide arc. Breathe the circle into full size, and then shrink it to a dot. Do this a few times so that you have a fairly strong image in your mind.

As you breathe, allow yourself to "see" this center of power. Spend meditative moments in this space, and think of stillness. Feel calmness, let there be no fear, worry, or even joy. The aim is to manufacture an unchanging nucleus of self. A self that ebbs and flows with exterior efforting, but basically remains unperturbed.

You should first begin by walking. Stand up, and begin keeping the visualization as constant as possible. Walk at least 50 to 100 yards. "Soft eyes" can keep your focus inside. If the place of stillness disappears while you are walking, go back into meditation.

The purpose is to use this sense as a biofeedback, running only when you sense the presence of the still circle. When the image fades, you will feel the necessity of recapturing the "feeling."

When you feel in touch, begin shuffling while holding the image. If you can maintain the image, go into a fresh swing tempo. If you lose it completely, or if the image does not appear for quite a bit of time, go back into meditation. You can do this on a large grass field or on the road, finding places for rest. When you finish, lie on your back, breathe into your abdomen, and visualize yourself breathing out your fingertips.

Searching for a Path with Heart

You are embarking on a journey that could change your life. It may have been a long time since you really felt robust and energetic. You believe a physical fitness program could become an addiction and make you, as well as your family, feel more secure, substantial, and healthy. You are practical and need to know how much energy it will take, what havoc it might wreak on the rest of your busy life.

Physical training pays dividends: Brightness will replace fatigue; there will be a place to ward off your tension; you will learn to play the edges of your physical abilities and deal with muscle pulls, stress, and mental ennui. If your involvement deepens, fun runs, local races, and the discovering of your own mental processes may ensue. The flavor of your life will change. The journey will be forever changing. It is the same for me.

In the midst of writing this book I was to run in the Boston Marathon. Over a three-year period I had regained my form as a distance runner, and in 1976 ran a 2:37 (26-mile) marathon. It made me believe I could run under 2:30 which I had never done even in my "peak" years. I also felt the need for personal success ir competitive running. As a running teacher, I feared becoming a comic who jokes people into fitness. I worried a critic might smirk and say, "Yea, but he never runs in the big races."

Also, my running experience is competitive racing. I know there is a chasm between athletics with a consciousness orientation, and traditional sports. In my own practice, and in my teaching, I want to bridge that gap.

After 20 years of athletics I am just beginning to find the range of techniques that can aid in the fullest expression of mind-body interaction. I want to share with you some of the events, and also the fears and frustrations that are leading me onward.

After I ran the 2:37 I began training occasionally with world-class marathon runners. My body is not really built for marathon running: I have a miler's musculature and fragile tendons. My motion is not especially fluid over 26 miles, but I do have excellent concentration. I began running on Sundays with Ron Wayne, a 2:16-marathoner. We would run 22 miles on the streets near his home in the industrial section of Oakland, California. The environment might seem like unpleasant surroundings, but the advantage is that instead of having to jump on and off residential curbs there are 3- to 4-mile stretches in which you can run smoothly in a constant rhythm.

I began to experiment with my running consciousness. The intensity of the workouts seemed to sharpen my perception. I would run with my eyes half closed, enabling access to my own dreamy world. If the road was flat and long I could actually take 10 or 15 steps with my eyes completely closed. I discovered that the strain I thought I was feeling was largely imagined. Further scanning pinpointed a few sore spots, but not overall fatigue. Then I would alternate opening and closing my eyes, or keeping my eyes "soft." In this state all I could see was Ron's shadow. I continued mainly inside for 20 minutes or so, and then opened my eyes wide while visualizing being hit by a pail of ice water.

On another run with Ron I had the sensation of going inside his body. It happened more by need than imagination. We were running 22 miles one Sunday, and I

Paul Bragstad

was coming down with a cold. For 12 to 14 miles I felt awful. Then a malaise overcame me, and for a few seconds I could feel myself actually going inside my running mate. Then the sensation increased. I felt like I was absorbing Ron's energy. I wasn't feeling my own body very much, and my desperate need for rest seemed to be progressively satisfied. I felt strangely attached to Ron. Each mile was easier, until after three miles I was refreshed and finished the workout in strong form.

My friend and colleague Jim Hickman is a researcher in parapsychological phenomena. I related the story to him, and he said it rang of truth. He asked me some leading questions, and was convinced that a strange transference of energy had transpired because my body needed it, and I had been experimenting with these new channels. Ron and I discussed the event and put it aside as an example of "staying with" or "in contact" with another runner. We had just about let go of the experience until Brian Maxwell, another world-caliber marathon runner wrote down a similar happening while running against Ron in the Seaside, Oregon marathon a few weeks later. The result was a 2:14.43-marathon:

> My thoughts focus on Ron in front of me. I stare down at a point just above the back of his knees. His stride is very close to mine and I can draw on his rhythm, adjusting instinctively to the slight variations in pace he makes. My eyes are fixed on the point above his knees—and my mind clears, settles, seems to separate itself from the activity that my whole body is concentrating on. I'm no longer conscious of the farms and houses and trees that we're passing—there's just the movement, my own and that in front of me and the discomfort and pain in my stomach is just a presence.
>
> We're back on the highway again—that much I'm aware of by the presence of a white line on my left. I'm in an almost hypnotic concentration, when suddenly I experience a split second of sheer disorientation and I snap out of it soon enough to realize that we've turned sharply to the right and onto another side road. I had

almost run up Ron's back and his quick movement in turning had thrown off my concentration, but we're safely around the bend and I go right back into my trance... then suddenly, I'm out of it again, but time and distance have passed because it's the 10-mile mark and they're calling out the time 51.37...51.38....

I was having interesting experiences. But I was losing myself, straying always from my own *dharma* (path). I would get excited before running with Ron, feel good or adequate during the training, but a strange soreness entered my body. I was getting away from myself a bit, and running tired all the time. I wanted so much to go step-for-step with Ron but I knew I would be doing myself a disservice. A person has to play the edges of his own physical ability, not just throw in with the bunch and see what happens.

Like most "serious" distance runners I am often running with soreness. Like a car going without oil, we sometimes just keep pushing till the whole thing falls apart. What I need is relaxation when the numbness or soreness in my legs sets in. Sometimes I go out and run hard, trying to run away from it.

My body was a stranger to me the month before the Boston Marathon. One day Michael Murphy had a group at his house to meditate. After 30 minutes all my pain went away through the camaraderie of the group and just letting go. Relaxation is so underrated.

On April 18, 1977 I ran in the Boston Marathon. A bad day for me. Running most of the downhill course in a fog, a pain in my side. All my plans laid to waste: I had had a successful workshop in Atlantic City with its boardwalk and friendly senior citizens. Then, the mistake of making a journey to my eastern seacoast roots. Visiting long lost relatives, trying to get by the alienation. It is too difficult for me to be accepted.

The night before the marathon I felt okay. But I felt the paranoia I get when traveling to the East Coast; the alienation entered my bones, muscles, tendons, and nerves. Scared about the race for a month, I trained stiff and anxious. Boston was my way of blending my ideas with my performance. I had the idea that I cannot be authentic unless I blend teaching with performance.

My festive feelings at the start became a dreadful nightmare. Never able to relax, no running partner, no connection. Just running blind on instinct.

A lift at 13 miles at Wellesley. Rows of women. In tradition, they yell in a chant that we have reached the halfway mark. I'm running through lines of pretty girls, trying to pull some energy from them. Nothing lasts long, and I'm sick on cobblestoned, tavern-lined streets.

I know for sure now that the run will be dreadful. The side cramp has given way to cramps in my calf and thighs. No amount of struggling or relaxing will do any good. I seem to hear voices in an undertone saying, "Boston, Boston." I must be going crazy.

An old friend Hugh Sweeney comes by talking to someone. A whole flood of runners stream by. The times at 5 and 10 miles are decent, but they have exhausted me. I look up at a city clock 1:35 and still at least an hour more to run; I have begun to die. No conjuring, no visualizing will help. I have tried all my tricks and now I am just an old car breaking down. I have television interviews about my book tomorrow—what will they say if I don't finish? My body feels like a machine—one part holds out, another breaks down.

One minute I am moving right along, the next I have stopped. I stop. Stop! *Stop*—the demise of a long-distance runner. I sneak into an office building, and peel off my shirt, which was the wrong one to wear. In shock: a combination of relief, guilt, common sense, anguish and frustration all hit at once.

Take a taxi home with another runner. Go pick up my bags. Just about faint in line waiting for my bag of gear, walk to the hotel dejected and out of sorts. Trying to clear my mind from the catastrophe. The world seems black, used, too efficient. I want it to be much later. Nothing now to do but survive and remember that it is sometimes beautiful. I know I have learned something, only time will make clear the whole message. Home weeks later. I got through the days after okay. Even did a talk show with Bill Rodgers, the most notable dropout of that Boston Marathon. He had read *Beyond Jogging*, and had tried the surge. It felt good being on television, and I had it worked out about dropping out of the race. Most were sympathetic, no hostility.

I had been home about a week when I made a big change in my personal approach to running. I had spent the morning with Ken Dychtwald, a body-person who specializes in teaching yoga to elderly people at the project he directs called *Sage*. Ken was going to get me flexible, but it would take time. I was sick of having sore tendons, whatever the reason. I also wanted to free myself from the recurrent dream of being in prison, to be more rounded, to have running as the core of my own *shanna* (mystical quest), to add yoga and other forms of stretching as well as meditation. On the same day, I went for a beer with my friend and meditation teacher Michael Murphy. We sat by a pier in Tiburon, California, and watched people as they came from the ferry, out of the business sections of San Francisco.

I had avoided a serious meditation discipline. I would go on and off the inner path. That day I made the pledge to meditate 20 minutes twice each day. I would start by observing my thoughts, paying attention to my breathing, and finding out more about my internal process. I didn't run that day.

Since that fateful day I have changed my running habits. Ken has developed a set of exercises for me that works on my difficult places: especially lower back, and pelvis. I have done a 3-hour set alternating between hot tub soaking and stretching. I have improved quite a bit in only 2 months—8 inches closer to the floor!

I meditate twice a day. Watching my thoughts,

concentrating on restlessness, thinking about detachment. I have developed a mantra to use while I am running. Last week I ran for hours through the woods chanting and observing my thoughts. Already I have had moments of new integration, days in which soreness doesn't set in after hard workouts.

In competition, the stretching and meditation has begun to help. Recently I won a 4-mile race over difficult terrain. Exactly the kind of footing that always gave me trouble. I used to get into an anaerobic state, and not be able to recover. At one point I got lost for a few moments. When I rejoined the front runners I felt tired. For a split second I "saw" myself finishing third. The thought entered my consciousness, and I rejected it. I caught it before it could come in. In another couple of strides I had regained my form and bolted towards the front. After a downhill I sprinted into a 600-yard flat stretch. I needed sprint form in the last 100 yards, but I held on to win. I wasn't as sore the next day as usual. I had found a new way of reacting with my body.

Beyond Six Weeks—
We Are All Growing

For six weeks you have followed a prescribed plan. You are probably worrying what to do from here.

To begin, let's review what you have accomplished, what knowledge you and your body have acquired. If you have followed the plan, you most probably improved in the mile or six-minute effort. You probably noticed that in the time assessments you used few of the special gaits. You will have noticed, though, the metabolism you have been practicing in the intervals took you through the "gears" of the assessment. Instead of transcendent thoughts you were experiencing fear, nausea and "blackouts." A few moments after a hard workout or time trial your "condition" returned to normal quite quickly. On some of those evenings you may have felt as wonderful, light, and God-like as you can ever remember.

Six weeks have passed and you are wondering—where do I go from here? Now do I become a jock?

My initial recommendation is to wait a day or two to make new plans. Run or don't run, stretch or don't stretch. Do inner exploration or go on a retreat. Leave yourself open for a few days and then review what you have learned.

You have learned a sense of pace. At first, when you started running between a 20 and 40 percent effort, it didn't mean much. Soon you were able to tell your range quite easily. You found the edges of your flexibility, and noticed the connection between tightness and how your body responded to specific workouts. The consciousness techniques brought relaxation. The style of movement alleviated lots of the boredom, and the breathing patterns gave you an awareness you had not been familiar with. You can follow the stream of your breathing, and the information about anaerobic metabolism has alleviated fear.

If you were pleased with the mile effort, move up one level. Remember that you are running with a ratio of 65 percent endurance, 25 percent speed or tempo, 10 percent resistance running. This ratio will keep you improving. If you want to stay with the mile, which is a balance between aerobic and anaerobic metabolism, some of the following suggestions will be helpful:

1. Don't let the running be a trap. Most importantly, stay with your own awareness.

2. Move up one level in the charts. Keep to five days a week. Begin to make up your own workouts. Follow your instincts.

3. If days go by when you can only shuffle, don't despair. Don't worry about being precise. Plan ahead for a "time spell" when you can get back into it.

4. Don't neglect the stretching and meditation practice. You need it for health and for roundedness. You need these approaches to make the running transcendent. You need to look inward before you can use consciousness while moving. Start with simple observation of thoughts, and move into an awareness of your breathing and into more subtle techniques like stopping your thoughts. In stretching, work out a routine and stick to it.

If your goal is to train to run longer than a mile, here are some suggestions. Extend the long runs and make them slower. Make the fartlek sections longer, but run them at slower paces. Play with the intervals—make the volume greater and the rest periods shorter. Do resistance and speed work a bit more sporadically. Generally, let the workouts be longer and have less intensity.

If you would like to be a sprinter, go slower on the long runs, add sprint form practice and do fewer intervals, but make them faster with longer rest periods in between. Fartlek workouts can be done on the grass areas near the track. Long slow running is just to keep general, overall conditioning. Your main purpose is to learn to run without oxygen over a short distance. Mentally rehearse being fast. In your life, act relaxed. Sprinters walk slow and run fast.

See your conditioning, the act of running, as part of a new lifestyle. Follow the new habit, and the addiction will take care of itself. Most of the time you will not have to extend yourself to go farther or faster, it will just happen as a result of your training. If you have wholeheartedly gone through the six-week plan, it will not be very difficult to keep it up, to have it become part of your lifestyle. Good luck and happy trails.

A Six-Month Program—
the Pleasures of Ritual.

In the fall of 1976, Esalen Sports Center created a six-month program to disseminate information, especially about running, meditation, and flexibility exercises we had been developing in workshops and in our personal training. Thirty-two people signed up for what was to be called the Mind/Body Development Program.

At that time Esalen still maintained an office in San Francisco and we were beginning a legacy of being the first long-term non-residential program. We were enthusiastic, a little too excited at our first meeting. I addressed the group, talking cautiously about the will and perseverance it would take to last out the time we were committing to each other. I could sense the lovely days of fall in San Francisco but I knew we would also mutually face the sudden arrival of winter, and the end of daylight savings time.

It was a group of high intelligence. Most had an understanding of Esalen and the human potential movement. Most were not in top physical condition. Lovely male and female faces with bodies that carried extra pounds. People distressed in sweat outfits, worried about feeling like jocks. They wondered why sports don't seem like the mystical journey they had been reading about. They were looking for secrets and short-cuts.

Some arrived in street clothes. They knew nothing of the athletic culture. Transcendental running, feeling good while running around the block was, for them, an illusion. Getting a glimmer of health would be acceptable to them.

Among the group were five of my long-term students. They were already into their physicality. They joined this class for a group experience. They want to extend the possibility of spiritual running. They would be steadfast throughout the program. My enthusiasm for their progress would ebb and flow. I took their physical condition personally.

Barbara Hazilla was my co-worker. She has a way of teaching flexibility exercises while allowing a person to maintain a deep state of relaxation. I can also count on her when interpersonal issues arise. She has been trained in a psychological discipline called *Psychosynthesis*.

My main sensation again is caution. I pointed out the ironies of physical culture. I played down psychological vows in favor of plain, old fashioned stick-to-itiveness. I want people to have a vision of the future, and not look up too much.

I explained that ahead of us were ninety sessions which would focus on running, flexibility exercises, and consciousness exploration. The consciousness work will include meditation, visualization, and guided imagery. Special visitors will introduce new methods and techniques. The *sensi* (a word given to a master teacher in martial arts) of Aikido from San Francisco, Robert Nadeau, would teach us how to apply the methods of energy awareness, using the force attached, but outside, the body to gather power in sports like running.

George Leonard, besides being a wonderful teacher, is a theoretician. In his book, *The Ultimate Athlete*, he places the meaning of sports in the personal growth of the individual. He considers himself a transformationalist, and has written a book entitled, *The Transformation*. The term refers to his feeling that the world is at a serious juncture, the next epoch will bring transcendence or destruction. George's hope is that our culture is leading towards an evolutionary period of austere spirituality.

Transformational sport means that the doer is a seeker, the coach a guide, the activity a preparation for our further development as human beings and as a race. The change in our lifestyle will by necessity bring us closer to our bodies. Physical fitness is not just a way to make our bodies feel better. Mind with body, a psycho-physical orientation, can take sport to the new level.

When I begin a group, I start by having people run only 80 yards at a time. In this way, if someone falls back they can catch up during the rest period between runs. During these first workouts, I observe the levels of fitness in the group; it is like scoring a piece of music. You can anticipate the blueprint and the result it will bring. It is the steps towards that blueprint that now have to be worked through.

On the first nights we would finish the sessions by "sitting" on the seawall, an expanse of block-granite steps that lead to the sea next to our green. Sometimes in guided imagery meditations I would transfer images through the din of the waves. If the sound of the sea became too loud, I would release the group and have them observe sounds of the breaking sea.

In the beginning it was raw enthusiasm. We could have developed an accountability that included a pre- and post-assessment in areas such as exercise physiology, creativity, flexibility. We didn't do this (although I would now), and attendance became the only means of judging program effectiveness. During the months of December and January when attendance fell off, I often felt impotent to make my ideas a reality. Barbara, my co-worker, got me through many periods of seeming failure and feeling defeated.

When you begin teaching something in the human potential movement, it is probably a journey from avocation to vocation. I had been a runner for fifteen years. I began teaching from the ideas that had become part of my own personality just from being inside the running culture for so many years. My method of running and of teaching grows by new experiences. The comedian Bob Hope tells a story about early vaudeville in which comics would polish the same act in city after city. It is the same in developing a way of teaching. You try things, and when they work you refine them and add new things, trying not to make them embellishments. When Michael Murphy first taught me ideas, they lacked emotional content. Ninety sessions gave me a lot of room for experimenting with the group.

When I first began teaching I fell back on my own running. Presently my own running is the place for my experimentation. Breathing, visualizing, combinations of new methods—I try them on myself. I recently ran second out of 800 in a 5-mile race in 24 minutes, 52 seconds—faster at thirty-two than I could have been at twenty-two. I'm interested in new fields—psychic self regulation, flexibility, nutrition, forms of meditation, and exercise physiology. The programs grow as we grow as teachers and individuals.

If the first sessions were idyllic, a shock wave hit after daylight savings time ended. The group diminished. Some came upon medical and personal problems. Others couldn't keep the commitment. In the first month we lost five people. Overall at least one third of the original thirty-two never made it to the last sessions.

If you were to trace six months in anyone's life it would be full of ups and downs, injuries, personal difficulties, periods when the training schedule is a good part of your life, other times of fatigue and failure. It is a life's cycle and no one escapes it—beginner or world class athlete. When the six months were finished, those left, a hard core of 15, remained close friends and decided to keep training together. We groped for a way to keep our connection. Many were in the finest physical condition of their lives—able to run six miles, some losing fifteen pounds, etc. The group decided to meet once a week. I was willing, but two things needed clarification. I needed a spiritual orientation, and a time trial for the mile so that I could tell what we had accomplished in six months. We picked a target date for the mile run, and everyone agreed. This is the story of that ritual, that run.

The Mile

It drizzled today in Marin county. We had been having drought conditions for two years, but it rained today. All the old-timers are walking around in rain coats with expectant grins. Everything that has been dry is receiving mist.

If you run, you come to love these days. The oxygen seems more accessible to your lungs. The ions from the heavy clouds are said to release energy. The running track is moist; you seem to make tracks like initial steps on snow.

Today is our target date at Tamalpais High School in Mill Valley. Fifteen had survived the six months of darkness and cold. Tom was one of my favorites in the program. He is a lawyer who runs a bar called Finnegan's Wake. At our first meeting Tom wore street clothes. He had never run and had no inclination towards physical exercise. Chubby but leprechaun-like with an intellectual high forehead, pasty Anglo-Irish skin, a set jaw, and comic-sad eyes, Tom literally plugged through the first few months of workouts. He was not distinguishable in running but in social interaction he had a definite character. If we had to change the place of a workout Tom would stand like a traffic director channeling everyone to the right location. If only a half dozen came for practice Tom would be one of them. Near the end of the program I gave him my old watch as a memento of his enthusiasm and perseverance. In some ways there is more joy in coaching a Tom than a potential world-class athlete. I'd rather reconstruct a '64 Chevy than fine tune a racing Porsche.

Stan at forty-six had smoked a pack a day for many years. Now he doesn't smoke or drink, and at forty-seven was whizzing around the mile run with the rest of us youngsters. Steve is a successful businessman who finds executive talent for large companies. He was primarily interested in the spiritual aspects of running. He had always had loads of athletic talent, but shied away from knowing what he could run for a competitive effort.

David is a handsome, muscular man who was hesitant about joining the program because he was a homosexual. Before he signed up, he discussed the feeling with me. I told him it didn't matter at all to me. We never spoke about it again, but it always stayed in the back of my mind. It seemed like he was always competing with me, but I couldn't tell if this was my own projection or not. He always seemed to be trying to catch me into admitting I had not kept my part of an agreement. On one of the last days of class he chose me as a partner in a "trust exercise" in which two people press their backs to each other and either take command or surrender to the other. I could feel a bond between us that was born, it seemed, from our training together. It might have had some sexual overtones. I wondered whether physicality changed the situation for him.

Bruce owned a company that paints houses in Victorian style. A 5'3", 116-pound jackrabbit he began the program somewhat in the middle fitness category. In a mixed group of men and women, he had clearly become the most fit person in our group. He had spent months in India meditating, and is as flexible as any male yogi I have ever seen. I want Bruce to become a teacher of my method. Our problem for a time was he was too obsequious in our relationship. Perhaps when I am sixty I can have that kind of a relationship. At thirty-two the only way I can work is as mutual friends.

Silvia has lovely facial features, and a sparkling personality. She, like many young women who are not especially athletic, had let herself relax into a weight problem. She carried delicate features on a buxom body. On one of our first guided imagery sessions she became aware that her relation to her body was one where she had always wanted to look good for others rather than feel beautiful herself, inside. When she realized that she ate frequently out of her hostility of having to please others, her weight came off and in 1977 she ran the 7.8-mile Bay-to-Breakers cross-city run in San Francisco.

Andy is Silvia's lover. He went through similar changes. They both had changed their diets, restructured personal activities, and arranged times running together which were marvelous interchanges.

Thom and Debbie were gallant throughout. Susan and David are both doctors who had to miss many workouts because of work commitments. They were to run strongly and courageously. Cynthia was the most improved runner, and she came early and ran her mile. Norma was courageously recovering from recent surgery. She was to cover the mile in under 10 minutes.

Michael Murphy and I go for our customary noon-time run. There is a slight drizzle in the air, we are buoyant. I have been experimenting with lots of stretching and meditating rather than logging 100 miles a week. I am beginning to identify myself more with being a coach than a runner. A time trial for 12 people is something I have never done before. I somehow feel I know what shape people are in by watching them run during workouts. But do I really know the times they can run? Michael asked me what I thought people might run today. "Well, I thought, Bruce can run 5:05." "Really?" said Murphy. "He would be a perfect person for me to race against." It was left at that.

Everyone arrived at the proper time. Murphy had agreed to lead us through a five-minute meditation before the mile run. Five minutes of inner looking before the ritual ordeal of a mile run. "Let the exuberance fade from your awareness," said Murphy. "Get into a calmer readiness and acceptance." We sat with this mental image for five minutes. It felt right going into the event from solemn rather than unbalanced glee.

At the starting line the group looked remarkably like any other group that gets to the starting line for a race. My only instruction was to "be moderate."

Thom zoomed out ahead of everyone passing the 220 mark in 33 seconds. It seemed appropriate that the event would begin with a runner's most common error—going out too fast. By the end of the quarter-mile Bruce had jackrabbited into the lead. As Bruce passed the quarter-mile in 72 seconds it was beautiful to watch his stride. Michael commented, "Do I look that fast going around the track?" Amazingly, in different situations, a four-minute mile can look slow and a five-minute mile fast.

I became absorbed in watching the faces on the field as they rounded the bend coming out of the first lap. The group had logged many miles over the last six months. The few who had missed workouts, gone away on trips, they would suffer the most. David looked younger than I can ever remember. He seemed to be recapturing his youth. Steve looked like he had done this many times before, falling comfortably into his pace, seemingly not fatigued. Andy ran with a fierce determination, head cocked to one side. Silvia looked lovely. Susan ran with spirit. Tom and Stan were not to be denied their accomplishments.

I was very proud of them. They had weathered many months of uncomfortable training, and dark cold nights. But these had not only made them more resilient, it had added the mystical quality of an ordeal surmounted. Who could tell what experiences, workouts, were adding to this "assessment run"?

I did not give particular instructions about gaits or tempos. The body knows what tempo or gait is appropriate for the situation. It was the sustained discipline over the last six months, the fifteen miles a week that was paying off. I was joyful that they all seemed to be enjoying the experience. They all seemed intent on getting the most they could out of their bodies.

Bruce went through the half mile in 2:29. Steve, David, Thom, Andy, and Susan followed. They were strung out, but not by much. Most had found their personal style and were running accordingly. The situation made more and more sense—people preparing themselves over a reasonable amount of time, running strongly within their capacities, expressing a deep intent for the completion of a commitment.

The group remained packed together. No one completely fell off the pace. Thom died a bit but struggled back. David was powering his way through the experience. Bruce was flying. Steve was running smoothly. Andy was determined. Silvia, Susan, Debbie, Tom and Stan were all going to make it fine.

The last lap loomed. Bruce hung in and hit the tape in my predicted 5:05. Steve ran 5:18 for the mile. Neither had ever run a mile for time before. I was as pleasantly surprised about the timings as anyone. Thom hit in 6:00, David in 6:01. Andy, who had six months ago been a chubby guy, ran 6:28. Susan ran 7:00, Silvia, Tom, and Stan all were well under 8:00.

Michael suggested we make our traditional celebration trip to the local bar. We sat as one family around a circular table drinking our beer and congratulating ourselves. Of course, it got a little rowdy. We were going to make Bruce run 120 miles a week, and lock him in a cell to become a lung-gom walker. Steve wasn't afraid of running time trials any more. David was curious about the young man I had seen on his face as he was gritting home. Silvia was glowing. Susan, our doctor, had been up all night, ran well, and now was soothing Debbie who had had a cramp after the run.

It was the ease rather than the times that impressed me. I felt like a full-blown coach (which is a little like the first time you have a baby). It seemed we had all changed a good deal during the event. In eight minutes they had all become runners, people with a unique record. I was sitting back, smiling, happy. This had really been my first graduating class. After the drinks, we poured out onto the streets, calling good tidings to all. We now had a record on our running shoes, and were given the freedom to say "I remember back in '77 I ran a mile. Boy, was I in shape then!"

A Psychic Occurrence

Running knowledge has saved my life. We all have periods in which our lives seem to go haywire. If I follow the thinking during my running sessions these times are likely to be excitable. I think I see various spirits, numbers, certain objects take on special meanings. In "white magic times" beautiful situations occur. Like the time I ran through Muir National Forest, and four people I ran past seemed to have a message for me. They were of different ages—a boy, a teenager, a man in his prime, and an old man. I sensed I was running through my own life in the energetic exchange that transpired. I had the feeling I had lived a life during the run.

These "good" occurrences stem from the aesthetic pleasures that are possible when the body moves in relaxed form and the mind, during heightened awareness, is receptive to these kind of experiences. But, there are darker occasions that make up another side.

Early in the summer of 1976 I was returning from an extended trip and visit to my home in New Jersey. I had learned the truth about the circumstances surrounding my father's death. I was tired and wired. I drank too much and turned my car over on a mountain road. Luckily I wasn't killed, but the accident began a strange series of events.

When the auto turned over the windshield broke, and I

fell into a state of shock. The car rolled in such a way that I was able to climb out one door. As I climbed out and got to my feet, a vehicle pulled up beside me. A man stepped out of a white van and offered to help. He offered to give me a ride to my home. I reported to the police, waited for them to arrive to get a report, and fell asleep in a frantic sweat, grateful for the service of this stranger.

The next morning trouble began to brew. When the strange helper returned to take me to see my car at the towing company he began taking control of me. He negotiated for my car bills, he told me when to drink my coffee. He commanded me not to call anyone about the accident. He made me drink milk as if I was drinking him. I sat like a "dead" man while people took glimpses of me and laughed. We drove to a trailer court located a few miles down the freeway. As we drove past the trailers women would yell out figures, "$5.25, $3.25." That was their price and a "master" of the situation could take what he wanted. The sounds in the stereo of my helper's white van were like the bleeting of bullets. I believed at any second I would be shot.

We returned to my beach apartment, and laying back on my bed he again commanded me not to contact anyone in the "outside" world. My wrist seemed broken; I felt helpless. Yet my only phone calls were to get us dates for the evening. I scurried through my phone book to call a special woman I had been wanting to see for quite some time. He told me he had been sent to take care of me by some old men in the Mafia, and that beefalo (half cow, half buffalo) were being sought by the Arabs.

As I sat in a fog the phone rang. He answered and handed me the phone. I was surprised he had not intercepted the call that was intended for me. It was an old friend, a teacher, Herbert Kohl. His voice was edgy and careful. He seemed to know the space I was in, and in the language he communicated he began developing a code in which he could give me information. He had me answer back to him the things he said, and got my voice pitch changing. I seemed to come back into my own personality. Later he would tell me that my "energy" was so low he could sense my emptiness. He said my voice originally was the voice of my possessor.

Herb's instruction was to have this person sign something, anything, so that there was a record he had been there. Herb explained that if I didn't do this someone would follow in this person's absence.

The acknowledgment of my situation gave me a tremendous boost. Survival energy began to stream through my body. I stood up and began stalking my possessor. He backed off and then threatened me. I was gaining impetus quickly. I shifted my tack. He wore a pair of what is commonly termed "cosmetic" running shoes. The kind of shoes that look authentic, but at half the price don't have the qualities of a top-rate shoe. I became a friend in crime, talking about the little things that can make the difference in tight situations. I convinced him that in a tight situation the cosmetic shoes would fail.

Under my bathroom sink is an array of shoes. A while back I had bought a shoe I thought I could race in, but I found they were flimsy, and that without any internal support a novice could not go far on them. They were flashy though, red with a sloping white stripe. I gave them to him. I had begun preparing for my battle by slipping on my Esalen sweat shirt and visualizing I was Marty Liquori (a champion runner from near my hometown in New Jersey who had missed the Olympics because of a leg injury). I put on my most trusted shoes, maneuvered towards the door and struck. I charged head first at him. He scurried down the trail outside my house, looking back at me smiling and laughing.

He hid behind a tree, but I was happy to chase him around and around the tree. My purpose was to keep him moving until he became exhausted. Finally he made a run for it, and as I chased him I could feel all my anger, frustration, and confusion finally being released. I let him run awhile without closing the gap. I finally collared him with a burst and a strangle hold. I squeezed his neck and punched the side of his head.

Everything gets frantic. He thinks it is a drug bust and begins looking up the street for intercepting cars. I become desperate about him signing the documents. I scream in a confused fashion. I will let him leave, but not until he signs the paper.

"Paul Pretzel has been here, and aided Mike Spino after his car accidnet." I let him go. He scurries up the road towards his van. In a daze I instinctively begin walking towards the Zen Center, a Buddhist meditation center near my home. I need to escape to sanctuary.

As I am on my way through the first gates, I notice a man hypnotizing a girl in a meadow. He looks my way, and I know he is the next oppressor unless I can break the chain of events that have me in bondage. Sounds, wondrous and melodious, reverberate in my ears and pull me backward. It is taking all my strength to move forward.

Pretzel's car passes on the upper road. He had said he was heading for Berkeley. It seems there are many cars on the road—they all seem new and shiny. A wonderful, luxurious smell enters my consciousness. The aroma stirs me to relax, lay down, become passive. In anguish I press forward seeking a human contact.

I jump two fences and am drawn to the sounds of light music coming from one of the cabins. The music frightens me but I have the urge to make contact, to trust someone. I have instinctively moved towards the main house of the Zen Center. I must trust them.

Paul Rosenbaum, the assistant *roshi* (teacher) greets me and I have the feeling he senses my state. We sit in the sun and I try to pour out the elements of the story. He calls the Murphys to come pick me up. Some Zen students are wrapping wire around the beams of a new structure, others are packing into a very dusty car with cardboard boxes stacked in the back seat. They are on their way to Berkeley.

Running into Spirit

We had spent the last two hours alternating hard fifteen-minute runs with periods of meditation, sitting on the grass by the seawall, emptying our minds of thought until we felt an energy to run again. During these two hours we had run some six or seven miles.

Now we were standing in sweat clothes at the counter of the little delicatessen. Having worked out hard like this for over fifteen years, I was completely recovered. A warm dilation was spreading through my chest and stomach, with a sense of well-being that more than made up for nagging injuries and periods when running seemed a dreary waste of time.

Michael Murphy, for whom a workout like this was a recent accomplishment, was experiencing something entirely different. It had started with a slight dizziness a few moments before that reminded him of a lightheaded feeling that sometimes came about six miles into a long, slow run. But now the feeling had grown more intense. That emptying-out we had practiced during our meditations had hit again, spontaneously, with sudden startling force. Was he going to faint?

He glanced at me. I was a reassuring point of reference. Then he sat down at a table and he tried to focus on the floor.

I sensed something was wrong with my friend and gave him a questioning glance. I went over to the table, and

Mike tried to tell me what was happening.

"Everything's unreal," he said. "But go ahead. I guess I'm still getting my energy back."

Sensing that the state would pass, I went back to pick up the lunch trays and ordered two beers. Now Mike felt a cold perspiration on his forehead and lips. This was not the usual change he felt after a workout like this. It was part fear and part contraction, it seemed, upon the rush of blood to his stomach. Moment by moment a sensation was growing that he was about to pass out.

But then something happened he hadn't expected. For an instant, the walls of the room seemed to vanish and there was nothing left but empty space. He was perfectly conscious of the people around him, perfectly in balance as he sat there, but the walls were gone and an emptiness stretched as far as his mind could reach.

Then space gradually contracted, and he sat there in a glow of relief. That sense of immensity, experienced a few times before during long hours of meditation, had given way to a reassuring sense of his friend and this lovely looking place. Later, when we had finished eating we talked about Mike's experience. It was, we concluded, an aftereffect of that intense two-hour workout.

For a year now we had been experimenting with workouts like this. I, then thirty, had been a nationally ranked runner in high school and college, and was making a living as a coach and physical fitness teacher for individual clients. Mike, then forty-three, had studied meditation and Eastern philosophy and was working on a novel, *Jacob Atabet*, that explored the kind of mind-body transformations we were trying to effect in our training. It was a good life when you could make the time for it, spending a part of each day working out, practicing meditation and trading notes about the lore of the mind in sport. But there was pain and weariness in it too, even moments of danger. Now Mike asked me if he might have had some kind of brush with a heart attack. He had already had one painful muscle spasm in his chest that had worried his doctor.

I reminded him of Bill Emmerton's experience during a non-stop run that lasted thirty-two hours. The famous stunt runner had felt himself slipping away into some other world, and for a while was carried along, he had said, by "the spirits of his ancestors." Charles Lindbergh had described the same kind of thing in *The Spirit of St. Louis*. During his flight across the Atlantic he too had started to cross over into a world of ghostly spirits that seemed to be wooing him away from the earth. There were hundreds of stories like these. Mike, in fact, had been collecting them for three years now in an effort to understand the undercurrent of mystical life that seemed to exist among athletes and sportspeople.

Fainting and dying. I *had* fainted a couple of times after a race, and felt a twinge of concern. Maybe I was working this older student too hard. "Let's lay back for a while," Mike said. "That was crazy today."

We had run most of those six or seven miles at something like a five-and-a-half-minute mile pace, and in spite of breaks to rest, Mike had never worked out like this before. "Yeah, I think you shouldn't run for the next couple of days," I said. "That was probably too much." Mystical experience or not, older runners sometimes had "cardiac accidents" during workouts like these. I had brought Mike along incredibly fast, I thought, down to a 5:15 mile now, and there was no telling how far he would go with all this mental training thrown in. But there were those "accidents." As Murphy drank down his beer, I watched him for signs of a wipe-out. I had once seen a friend pass out about an hour after a grueling workout, and the friend had been twenty years younger.

"It's strange," Murphy said, stretching back in his chair. "Do you think we did something wrong? It felt like I could override the pain altogether—like Richards and his friend." Practicing meditation, two yoga students we knew had stared at the sun for twenty minutes, burning holes in their retinas.

"There was an Irish runner," I said, "who ran 4:10 or something like that in his very first race and died about five minutes later. Maybe we have to look out." We both laughed and agreed that there had to be negotiations with "brother body." It would take more than will power to carry us along in our quest.

This was a conversation we had had every week or so that summer. Behind all the reasons we gave ourselves for this obsessive devotion, there was a secret exhilaration in pushing yourself to the limit.

Still, maybe we *had* gone too far today. Though the beer and the lunch were having a settling effect, there was something vaguely threatening about the state of his body, Mike thought. If he didn't maintain a certain kind of balance, things might collapse into bottomless space.... "Breathing," he said, filling his lungs for reassurance. "It must be the first source of pleasure. Breathing and beer." We clicked our mugs together in this sacred rite of runners. Breathing and beer could set you floating for hours. But underneath the camaraderie and warm dilation, he still felt the faintest trembling in his legs and that sense of a space reaching out further than his mind could encompass. It was a feeling that was reassuring and awesome at once, conceivably the taproot of all other pleasure.

How many runners felt this same thing, and then because of its strangeness turned away from it? Mike thought of the tentative, even bashful admissions all those veteran runners had made to him during the last several months. Were all of them skirting the edge of the void, like he was now, unaware or frightened by its power? Yes, they were, he thought, and their reactions were understandable. To have plunged any deeper during this past half hour would have meant a kind of death.

I read his thought and ordered us both another beer. We began to talk about the future. Each of us would set goals for the coming year, I said, trying to bring the focus down to earth. I would try to regain my college times in the two-mile, six-mile and marathon, and Mike would break his personal records in everything from a hundred yards to 26 miles. The beer had had its effect. Now I was declaring that I would run the marathon in two hours and nineteen minutes and have a crack at the Olympic team and that Mike would break five minutes for the mile! And we bought another beer on that.

We started planning future workouts. The dangers of this one were already fading. Sometime soon we would try running the three miles down Mt. Tamalpais from the West Point Inn in under twelve minutes; we had already done it in 12:30. That was one place where Mike could run with me, his coach, because when running downhill, balance and coordination are as important as strength. It was even conceivable that we could cover the middle mile on that grade in something like three minutes and 20 seconds, breaking the world record for the mile by half a minute! So what if the grade was something like six or eight percent? There are world-class milers we might beat on that kind of madness-filled run.

Then we would try an all-day session of jogging and meditation to see what would happen. By combining a marathon like that with the spirit of Zen *sesshins*, new vistas of our minds would break open. Hell, we could do it in a week—Mike could tell he was ready. It was amazing, Mike would later reflect, how quickly fear and pain would pass when a workout was over.

We continued, our minds reflecting dreamily on past workouts and runs of the future still to come. Runs to the Golden Gate Bridge around sunset, through sunlight and mist, across grass and asphalt and sand, skirting the swells on the beach while sailboats slipped into the harbor and fishing boats circled, gulls screaming all around them. It was a run to take a thousand times, and never would it be the same. Workout after workout jumped into view now, then the races still to come—with the Dolphin South End Club and at the all-comers' meets in the spring, at the Western Regional Master's and maybe at New York's

Van Cortlandt Park, where I had run in high school and college—a vista of running to fill the growing image of what we might yet discover.

"Do you think we might run right into some other world?" I mused. "Do you think we could just be running along, and after six or seven miles suddenly come out somewhere else?"

I had pondered this question several times of late, and always with a haunted look. "What do you mean exactly?" asked Mike. "What do you mean by 'some other place'?"

"I mean like some other *actual world*. We would be running along and, well, both of us would just disappear. It happened in a dream I had once."

"And where do you think we'd come out?"

"I don't know," I said, a distant look in my eyes. "Maybe on a beautiful planet in the constellation Orion. A planet with long winding trails in the mist. With purple peaks and skies. . . ."

"Or right into Big Mind," said Mike. "Like that time in Syracuse."

I had once run six miles along a slippery muddy road in a time that fell just a few seconds short of the American record. During that run I experienced my own encounter with death—for somewhere down that road I had felt the wind blowing flesh from my body until there was nothing left to resist the sweep through space. Something else had taken me, something grand and inexorable and powerful beyond anything else I had known. Then, when the run was over, I seemed to shrink back into my own body, and I had wept as I tried to decide "who I was"—the one who had run the race or the usual Mike Spino? That experience as much as anything else had led to my fascination with the psychic side of running and sport. When you let yourself go like I did that day, another kind of being might appear, something like that engulfing awareness the Buddhists called "Big Mind."

"Our run to the bridge becomes another world," Mike

said, remembering Zen tales. "Who needs another planet?"

"Maybe," I said. "Yes, maybe." Then a bright, slightly defiant look came into my eyes. "But you've got to admit the other way would be great. To run so well you were free to come and go from the earth. Just think of it, *big Mike!*" I said as I slapped my friend on the arm. "Just think of how it would feel!"

"Okay, coach," Mike said, smiling, but a little reluctant. "Let's go out and take a few steps."

So we stepped a little uncertainly into the afternoon light, expanded by three or four beers, and Mike stiff now from that workout leading toward the stars of Orion. "One day at a time," he said, limping toward his car. "Where'll we workout tomorrow?"

"At the edge of the planet—if you're ready!" I called, teasing and proclaiming at once. "We'll meet out there." I pointed toward the grass by the seawall. "Where the land disappears!"

Two Different Days in the Same Place

There is a tourist attraction eating and drinking establishment overlooking the San Francisco Bay where our group congregates after Sunday races at Lake Merced. Our group is made up of highly charged, complex individuals who release their energy through sporting endeavors. What they express is a microcosm of their world view. The hard running brings out the best of their sensations about the art of living.

On this particular Sunday morning, the group had just completed a 5-mile race against or with eight hundred others. Anyone could sense that everyone present was pleased with their performances as we raucously drank combinations of white, fluffy Ramos fizzes and imported beers. It was like a celebration of a gang of sinners who had just been through penance. For some it had been a difficult 5 miles, but now that it was complete we were free to let it all hang out. Michael Murphy, our teacher of innerspace consciousness, had run well—56th place and a 5:47-mile pace. I had watched him charge towards the finish line inside a wave of young runners. He had a strange look of surprise and satisfaction. It was not the spite of winning over others, but more the satisfaction of a person experiencing joy in a new activity. This sensation comes both from wonder at a new achievement, and the transfer of other life situations.

Dulce Murphy, Mike's wife, was a bit back in the pack.

She had been somewhat ill of late, and the race experience redoubled her motivation to get back into the discipline. George Leonard, our theoretician, was there. He was beaming, making grand proclamations. He had run just about even with Susan Mitchell who, taking up running at forty, had already run a 6:22 mile in a few months. She was writing a book about running and love, and was "into" the romantic sensibilities of the experience. Susan's children, who ran for the local high school, made a credible showing. The family feeling among us had a sense of union and freedom from the sometimes boring weekend family life that can set in on busy households. Jim Hickman and Mary Payne were also sharing the celebration. They are both special people. Jim is a parapsychologist, an investigator of psychic phenomenon. His main interest is in changes that occur in people's bodies through physical activity. The modalities, the sum of influencing agents, might deliver information about human possibilities. Mary has taken to running with great enthusiasm, but originally worried about failure or how she was measuring up to the others. After a few months she overcame this fear, and a serenity has slowly taken over her running. In this, her first race, she did so well I gave her one of my favorite shirts, a momento from the Hawaiian Marathon clinic.

My epic on this day was as strange as the rest. I had been teaching at health spas—the Golden Door and Rancho La Puerta in San Diego and Mexico. During the four days I taught at these spas my physical condition would feel wonderful and then terrible. One day I would feel fine, running through the Tecate, Mexico streets with a group. We would have fun by stopping half way to meditate in a Catholic church during the morning mass. Other days a soreness and numbness would set into my legs.

When I returned to the Bay area, I rested for two days before the race, and still the numbness persisted. During the warm-up and the actual running it was the same. Eight hundred people started the race, but I got out early, and after a few hundred yards was running among the leaders. The person running in first place made a surge for the front and I let him go, concentrating on second place. At 3½ miles it became easier. With only 1½ miles to the finish, I started to visualize myself as Ben Jipcho, the unbeatable Kenyan, but settled on Tracy Smith who had been a friend and outstanding performer on the Santa Monica Athletic Association teams back just after my days of college running. The picturing of Tracy worked and I was pulling space on the runner in front. I closed the gap on the front runner and finished second.

The race had been an interesting process. At the beginning I did an energy ritual taught by Robert Nadeau, the Aikido teacher working with us on energy awareness exercises. I became aware of two locations inside myself. I chose my lungs and the small of my back. Four or five minutes of this preparation shut down rambling thought patterns. By depriving the mind of rambling, I was able to prepare it for larger aspects. When free association took over, it gave the sense of traveling downhill in a stream or being carried up the road by a conveyor belt. This mental set was one I wanted to begin the race with. I find that the "kibitzing" done on the starting line wastes lots of energy. I'd rather be quiet in my pre-race activity, go inside and "set" myself for the upcoming journey. Even as I write these words I can recall the feeling of excitement in the contest. A butterfly begins in my stomach. Awareness in relation to our physical body is an area so little explored. The same was true about meditating on the numbness in my legs, and discovering that in the bottom of my abdomen was an open, loose space, while the rest of my body felt tight, as if it was holding on. I was able to expand the area of openness to include my whole abdomen and my legs became less numb.

Back at the Cliff House we were still going through the post-race analysis and basking in the exuberant energy that seemed to flow everywhere. Amidst talk as to what color we should have for our team clothes, what symbol reflected our intentions, George expounded on the perfect symmetry he saw in the assembled group. We had all done relatively close to our potential, we were congenial as to our attitude about the sport, and the raucousness of the group was a sure indication that we were alive and kicking—more animated after the hard five miles. As we closed the session, walking a bit tipsy from the fizzes and beers, the warm sun baked into us. Each of us had lived a nice experience to store in our memory bank, a beautiful memory of running and camaraderie.

Two weeks later, same scene, but a different setting. At Lake Merced eighty or so master (over forty) runners were assembled with serious set jaws and tones of traditional competitiveness. This race had a quality very different from the loose gaiety of the week before. The weather was also different. Wind gusts blew at gale force, some estimated at thirty or forty miles per hour.

When I arrived, the group was just heading out the main passage lane for the 5-mile loop around the lake. I pulled my car to the side, studied the group and found my friend Michael Murphy near the front of the pack. I scanned the field and saw he was in a good position. "Mike!" I yelled. He acknowledged me with a glance and a finger shake. I jumped back in my car and headed around the lake so I could have a vantage point from which I could view the group at mile intervals. It wasn't until I jumped from the car the second time that I sensed what kind of a day it was. Gusts of wind swirled, and the gloss that surrounds events where superlative performances occur was totally absent. If in our gleeful moments running is an affirmation that highlights the perimeters of life, these stark days force out our intentions. These kind of races are brutal tests at times. They can keep you introspective for days. They probe at the basis of your personality, and can be as debilitating as a terrible sexual experience. The sense of emptiness that follows a day in which you didn't quite give your all, haunts. Sometimes this emptiness is responsible for you "killing" yourself at crucial parts of racing. All the introspective suffering your mind does plays on you as you run the race over a dozen times in your head.

Michael was just beginning racing, and at 46 was actually a high school sophomore in his racing experience. At two miles I could see it was going to be one of those murderous days. He would have to half-kill himself to feel satisfied. Once as a high schooler I had faced a similar incident and ended up in an oxygen wagon, my thin body exhausted by the gusting winds. I could see it coming, but as a coach what does one do? I tried my best, but you could see the runners being battered around by the wind. Only the most experienced would survive. By surviving, I mean running a poor time and being content to finish well, or to give the effort up for a later happiness.

The third and fourth mile Mike held on to his position except for a few who came by him. Strange how the previous week all the jerseys had meaning, and the individuals had personalities. Wherever they finished, they were interesting. Today the winner would be just another person running down the street. There would be a crowd of about forty instead of three hundred waiting at the finish. No one would stand around afterwards talking about the race. The happiest would slip into their cars and get away as fast as they could. It was an absolutely no-fun race. Mike faded in the last mile and came in 18th. He had dreamed of finishing in the first five and had been in 9th place for the first few miles. Now it was just finishing, holding the pace, and surrendering to the pain for no reason. Fifteenth, sixteenth, what does it matter? For just a split second I saw a gleeful joker look on Mike's face, like a gambler might have after he had been hoodwinked and couldn't do anything about it.

Off again to the Cliff House for Ramos fizzes and imported beer. This time the atmosphere was filled with somberness, the feeling that something had transpired, something that was a necessary step, but still hard to swallow. Dulce and Claudia had run fairly well and were in moderate spirits; Paul, a photographer, was there with Corrine, Dulce's daughter. The gathering reminded me of a scene in the film *Fat City* in which the fighters have a hard one and sit around with broken noses, wrapped fingers bleeding, go over the fight, and out of frustration talk about all the things they are going to do once the tide changes. As a coach the melancholia, the stubbornness, the new intentions that set in on these days are part of the growth experience athletics can offer. I lived this time more fully than the previous session in which we had established a sort of perfect symmetry. Perfect symmetry or not, there is no traveling to the next dimension without these kinds of days. They are necessary, and like the first hard climb up a large and beautiful hill, you are happy it is behind you.

Mr. Weil

An academic who becomes a school teacher can run into trouble. He might be better off having a background as an usher in a rowdy movie house, or a short order cook in an all-night restaurant. Knowing a lot about math, coupled with a desire to help young people succeed in the world can sometimes be disastrous.

Mr. Weil was my homeroom and algebra teacher in the ninth grade. A dark thin man, he was prone to wearing blue suits that showed dandruff flakes from his close-cropped, kinky black hair. Bird-like when he spoke, he usually stuttered a bit. His blackboard writing was a chicken scrawl. He had a mania for not wanting to throw students out of class. He believed it showed on their records and made it difficult for them to get admitted to college.

The poor/good humble man should never have become a school teacher, especially not in a suburban high school where maiming the teacher is a mark of bravery. And he had the classes! Baby Sam had already driven two teachers to rest homes. Joe Dildo loved to take out his penis and show it to the girls. Every now and then someone would get punched out in the cloak room. Who was going to stop them?

With each succeeding week of the fall term, Mr. Weil's classes became rowdier and rougher. He still wasn't kicking kids out of class and attempts at discipline weren't effective. The word was around the school that you could do anything you wanted in Weil's class. No algebra was taught in math class, homeroom became a brawl scene. The assistant dean began coming to class to quiet us down. You could tell Mr. Weil's stay was doomed— *perhaps* he would last the year.

One Friday morning we had an assembly. Most students sat in the outdoor bleachers overlooking the football field and the running track. A few kids had taken to racing around the track. One race was in progress with the kids at least one third of the way around the 440 oval.

Out of nowhere bolted a thin, dark man in a blue suit. Within a few moments you could see he was catching up with the boys who were racing. The assembled students became remarkably quiet as we recognized the runner in the blue suit as Mr. Weil!

The boys were young and fast. Seeing Mr. Weil they accelerated. Weil closed on them, but at the last turn they pulled away to win. Weil continued at full effort stumbling to the finish line. Exhausted, he hung limply on the fence next to the running track. The kids in the bleachers cheered as if they were at a football game. Who was this person?!

Everyone liked Mr. Weil for a few weeks after that. But in a few more weeks it was all forgotten. The blackboard chicken scrawl alone was enough to exasperate anyone. By the end of the year he was gone. We really tried to like him. I remember a few kids saying, "Hey, Weil, that was a run for the roses."

Running is not an Easy Ecstasy

A runner is alone, looking out on the ocean's horizon. There's not another soul on the beach, and the void he feels inside spills out to surround and encompass everything. This sense of void already has lasted for weeks, and the confidence that his life was moving forward in a steady progression has diminished.

His present moments feel uncomfortable, the past empty. His personality has become vulnerable to the undertones of jibberish that has become a fashionable means of communication. The jabs of those near him enter his mind as he walks the streets or takes a solitary meal. Although running eases the ennui somewhat, down deep he has begun to question his identity.

He is growing older. Life's concerns are changing. When he runs at night, he looks into lighted houses. Lately, he has begun to wonder what it would be like to live there, though he believes he would have to give up the sense of peace his brand of physical activity delivered if he sought power in the commercial world.

For years, running has been his sport, his discipline. He has met many wonderful people, and has built a philosophy around the activity. But has he become dependent upon it? Though he believes the joy he occasionally discovers while running is an energy at large in the world, when he misses a few weeks of practice he feels a vast dissatisfaction, a deep void. The world becomes dull, and sadness overcomes him. When he runs he feels clean. His daily miles of running give him a basis upon which he defines his life, but, it also allows him to disregard vital concerns. What he needs to further his personal integration is a way of combining what he has learned from running with the information he missed by specializing, by seeking knowledge in a single way.

Within his own framework of seeking truth, he wants to find the balance, the harmony he sees emerging in those who recently took up running. He has found that when people first discover running, they do not confront the same inner complexity with which he is dealing. His own relationship with the activity goes deep into his being. He believes the issues dear to him could be vital for everyone, but he fears restricting or submerging the personal insights of others with his viewpoints.

It is early evening and the streets are nearly deserted, but the faint glow of the streetlights reminds him of a day recently when he had felt the wild joy of physical activity. After weeks of holding on to his running partners, content to last out the workouts, a new energy had overcome him. Instead of following in the pack, he took the lead with poise and style. He rarely joined in the small talk of their ordinary training, but recently he had been able to enter the spirit of the man who set the pace on long workouts. Instead of fighting off the fatigue, he drifted into the rhythm, the actual space of the pacemaker. Suddenly his mind was calm and a part of his presence diminished.

The remembrance of this time when things clicked and felt perfect is helpful. His consciousness is soothed and he now feels he can wait out this wave of worthlessness. His spirit is rediscovering a truth, his own worth, that it accepted at the deepest level of his being. Running has seduced him and like a magic lady it gives its potency in the strangest places, the most unlikely corridors. He knows the words he might use to express himself won't tell the whole story of the journey. His tale will miss the mark and leave the image of just another lost soul running down an empty or crowded street. What keeps him going is the promise of a larger deliverance. He realizes he has been on the path for many years, and he now has a satisfaction he did not discover in the painful first lessons. He has gone as far as anyone he knows, the spirit has made its initial tracks, but he needs to continue moving with the proper intentions. He carries the burden of finding valuable, worthwhile passageways, and he knows this quest can make him gleeful with passion or take him to his knees in depression.

Running and Love

Recently a workshop participant told me a story about an experiment which the Italian Olympic team tried. They set up two control groups. The first group was to live in the Spartan tradition: no lovers or wives, separate from the outside world. A second group was given free access to relate fully with the environment. It was found that on the night before competitive situations this group on an average drank half a liter of wine and made love. This second group did much better in competitive matches.

Ben Jipcho, the prolific Kenyan distance runner who has been the most successful professional runner of recent times, relates similar ideas. One evening, after spending a few hours talking about athletics, I asked Ben the lifestyle most conducive to athletic excellence. His reply was "Good sex, the right food, rest, and proper training." I asked him why he put the items in that order. "Because that is the order of their importance," he answered.

When I was a school boy I was nervous before races. I couldn't sleep at times, the race going through my mind. I particularly remember an early summer meet in which a runner older than I, Maurice Hobson from Texas Southern, was talking among friends about the beautiful women he had brought to the track meet. Maurice liked me and always included me in the "sense of feeling" he created at a track meet.

When he talked about where he had just come from, I

thought it was nice, but that he surely would not run well that day. He ran the fastest 880 of the season and seemed to have a smile on his face the whole way.

When I became older, and started to monitor my sense of my own physicality, I began to understand that a loving interaction with another human being in juxtaposition to an athletic event does something to the relaxation and calmness that is not exhausting, but revitalizing. This loving drains the tension from your being, especially if you allow yourself to release to that empty floating feeling at the core of sexual expression.

It is possible to take the exuberance of lovemaking, and move wonderfully into the deepest states of relaxation. Transferring this mellowness into running can be joyous. The depths of the soft, caring, touching way of being with another is diametrically opposed to dominance in sexuality: dominance, control, the master/slave relationship can serve as a screen to separate a person from their own bodies. This bondage can be released by touching on a deeper emotion, the blending of spirits made possible through physical exercise.

I am referring to this in the highest philosophical vein—taking the soul of another for the edification of your own ego. I don't mean the momentary surrender to a temporarily dominant force. Giving in to this tide of energy is part of the ebb and flow of any relationship. Be partners. Run, hike, swim, bike, spend a day in the country. Really feel what it is to get in touch with your body, to relate to another in a totally pleasurable sharing: Be carefree, light, do things insignificant and inconsequential. Play...play...keep the play of the day's activity in your loving. You'll see you don't need all the mental contrivances, and certainly not ropes, blindfolds, or humiliation.

On Being a Teacher

The most satisfying and effective teaching stirs new belief in the participant. This belief allows the person to think independently. The focus is independent thinking, the ability to act responsibly, and spontaneously. Many educational institutions proclaim these goals, but some models are more effective than others.

For instance, I once taught a group of sedentary people (defined in this particular instance as not having done any physical exercise for five years) for forty-five sessions over a fifteen-week period. The purpose of the project was to see if changes occurred in body chemistry. The goal was to find the sources of heart disease. The result was that the physical fitness of the participants improved 10 to 40 percent, but had little improvement in their overall body chemistry. Most could not escape the limiting body image they had created for themselves.

Was it that I was not able to free their inner-being? I tried.

The real purpose of physical fitness counselors is the greater struggle, dealing with the cerebral image. The teacher's task is to monitor the changes as a person navigates towards his own inner archetype.

We live in a culture starved for insight and improvement. We pay for and glorify organizations that offer packages toward this end. The tightest marketing and developmental scheme will produce the most money and influence the mass culture. This process, however, does not produce completed students. Especially outside the framework of schools and organizations, there are few ashrams, or ad hoc training groups committed to the full learning process, the change in archetype. I can't do it in forty-five one-hour sessions if my only purpose is transferring information about physical fitness. My need is to create a pathway.

I have been extremely lucky in being at the correct juncture to meet teachers who have shown me the way into my personal directions. Jack Scott taught me the technicalities of physical training, Mihaly Igloi taught me the effort necessary for success. Herbert Kohl gave me the belief in myself to write, Percy Cerutty taught me how to motivate people. Michael Murphy was Socrates, George Leonard shows me style and finesse. I watch these teachers mainly to learn about how to live life. They are parent figures for a while, and then we become associates.

The difference between the student and master is that the teacher's passion is more subtle, the depth of happiness or pain more complex, the ability for passiveness or near-violent energy more acute. And always the addiction to teaching, the love of watching anything—plants, people, organizations, concepts grow.

The teacher tries to take you beyond ordinary reality. What if you operated each day with the knowledge that the world is in a solar system that is ever-expanding and has no edge; that our bodies are made up of atoms that are not solid; that in reality we are non-solid bodies moving in a world that has no edge. For me it is more real to relate how people don't really change, but grow through trying. How the best we do together emerges as if it was born long ago—teaching is just a way of waiting out the cycle. To me, the ideal is a community of people striving with a common purpose. In this organization there is a hierarchy, the student must wait for information, but the discipline is done through an inner laughter.

Every sense of life has already been lived somewhere. The body changes each moment through the biological manufacturing of blood cells, the transference of oxygen throughout the body. The body is in constant change.

Being a teacher is a very high state. It is full of responsibility. A master teacher watches, and can be either a resource person or can awaken the energy dormant in the aspirant. The best teachers love the addict and the rebel equally. Only through the synthesis of opposing personalities does he weave the web that is his truth.

Growth weaves itself through all: the measuring, the striving, the total giving of oneself. A good teacher puts order and purpose into life. Often a unique student gives the teacher a special satisfaction. In the ideal of what their relationship can be, each locates the elements that make their individual existence rewarding.

The teacher grows by giving. He, as the student, yearns for a type of release, but the satisfaction is very different. It is the blending of purposes which creates an artful union.

Growing as a Coach

The methods set forth in this book can be used as shortcuts and means to greater athletic pleasure. Most of the methods and approaches are self-explanatory. But there is no doubt that a teacher giving detailed instructions can greatly aid your development.

Therefore, if you have always been fascinated by athletics or are into some aspect of teaching, this is an invitation for you to become a teacher. If you have the opportunity, teach someone. If you need a teacher, come to me.

My background was in teaching emotionally and educationally disadvantaged young people. When I think of my own teaching, it reminds me of a story Charles Lindbergh relates in *The Spirit of St. Louis*. He said it was easy flying the Atlantic after bringing the mail through the storms in small airplanes during the early years of aviation. When I first began teaching cooperative adults who were anxious to learn, I opened up. My own creativity expanded when I didn't have to spend so much time amusing and controlling the children.

In my early years of teaching I would sometimes race through instructions. I remember getting through all the information of a two-day workshop in the first morning. A friend, Lauren Eckroth, who operates the Natural Learning Center in Hawaii, told me, "Mike, slow down, people remember the nickel and dime words and ideas."

When I first taught workshops it was difficult to watch, to let things unfold. I was always afraid the group would get away from me; I'd lose control. If someone asked me a question I would not pay them full attention. I would talk in cliches, I had pat answers. A problem scared me, an unsatisfied workshop participant was a threat. If something wasn't getting through I'd raise my voice and act crazy. I didn't know the rhythm differences between lecturing and giving instructions. I relied too heavily on enthusiasm.

In slowing down, you find your own liberation. Rather than being exhausted, you share in the workshop participants' elation. You can be inventive on the spot. You think in larger modules, you can be more yourself.

Remember, no one can teach exactly like you. We can duplicate methods but not spirits. Yes, it is difficult not to feel competitive. We are all our own institutions—as a freelance teacher, coach, or any artistic professional.

If you are good at teaching something, stay with it. There will be many fads and crazes. They pass. All trips have limited markets. Find your own niche, give it your personality. Students will come if you have something to teach.

A few years ago I had only one student. His running was an extension of me. On a particular day now I might be coaching fifty people. Most are bodies without names. Over time it is the individualization of the person through the teaching that is exciting.

I want to give you the news—coaching, teaching, is a good life. Your fruit is the happy people who become your friends. There are phonies, competition, managers. But, if you stick, you'll watch yourself grow. Sometimes I might be speaking and say to myself, "Is this me, is this me?!" because a new part of me has made it to the surface. I click more and more of the time. The feeling is its own reward.

Running as a Madman

It rained today. My legs have a numbness that
    worries me. I watch them and try to learn
    a bit more about my own personal process.

Intermittent rain at times today, clouds swirling
    giving off incredible energy.

Cold, pelting rain today. Aside to running mate:
    Does this make us tougher? No, it only
    makes us cold.

Running in the rain today. Rain is Zen
    because it makes everything more
    ecstatic and grounded at the same time.

Rain makes me melancholy. Melancholy makes
    me think of dying. Will I be ready when
    it is my time to go over the rye?

A beautiful dying might be better than the
    current rat race. At a party drinking
    wine. Someone tries to drink wine with
    my wife. I want to take them on the street
    and torture them with running.

"Aren't you cute now, as your body disintegrates,
    piece by piece. How would you feel in situations
    where it didn't help to be cute, cynical or
    worldly?"

There is a lot to be learned by just putting one
foot in front of the other. I'd like to
take the whole smirkish world on a forced
march

And just at the moment when an inner accord
grows among them, lay under a rock and cry.

Running as an Anecdote

The morning held fog,
    every appendage took its turn,
Doing peek-a-boo with strain
    and pain.
The world gets funny when
    you quickly change direction—
You make a decision and
    hope for the best.
It's reflected in the consciousness
    of a morning run.

In the Fog of a Morning Run

In the fog of a morning beach run,
   the light burns off the elements
And a night's mental anguish becomes
   toned into the everyday.
The mind sometimes becomes garbled.

When the thoughts are not yet straightened out.
The running helps. Each one can
   bring you closer to who you are.

Even in the periods of rest, while waiting
for vague ideas to become direction,
the running is like returning home. Other
times it brings to the surface the inner
scatteredness and distraughtness.

Then, after the run, becoming wired,
   everything rushed to the surface,
My conscious home marred.
And I find myself reacting to everything. Not
   like an Indian who waits in the bush
   with a man's deliberation and responsibility.
Recovering from life's war zones takes time,
Quiet running at morninglight allows
   you to store back, finding necessary new
   selves and old land posts.

In the passing time the body automatically
   stores energy from the air and elements—
You can't help looking for omens, and a
   practical passageway.

All across the country an inner power is being
   unleashed.
With animal intensity, growing out of the battle
   of dogs and cats.
And this sense of intensity comes to each in his
   own way.
Life for each cannot be adequately named to another.

The hue of the color of a leaf moves me,
  not like it touches another.
The smell of someone loved catches me,
  and goes unnoticed by another.
Another is separate, living behind the
  veil that is me.

Children's voices in the distance are melodious
    to me.
The ache of separation from someone loved is death
    for me.
Taking a shower after a satisfying run lightens
    and lifts me.

Yet, somewhere back of the illusion of me is
an unfinished being—
I can't find the button that frees the inner
self.

Haven't yet discovered the balance of silence
   and explosion that will put all the elements
   together in one situation.
Still looking for a me that flows through existence.

Love Thy Discipline

Another day, sunrise, same as many other days.
Noticing the weather, but not especially.
Stomach rumbling, waking care-filled.
Introspective today. Sometimes happiness is
    as relaxed as a rambling boy/star.

Or discord, brittle silence, missed
    communications. Going over a conversation too many
    times.

Ice sets in. Composure shaken. Being stable emotionally
    is like teetering on the edge of the precipice.

Pioneering a new way of knowledge. All day, day
    after day: meditate, stretch, run, write, teach.

The world turns outside my cocoon. Peeking—
    see fast words, slick moves. People with
    alcohol smells, others hyper-clean thinking
    they know more than they do.

What if I were a screaming iconoclast? That is
    no way out of the dilemma.

So I: meditate, stretch, write, run, teach.

How can you make a lot of money and not be famous?

When I get out of debt will I feel like a man?

Millions have taken up running and I am a
 sought-out teacher.

Yet, I still churn inside and lash out when I'm uncertain.

Filling the world with red heat...people want
 clean energy! So I make them happy behind my
 mask as a running teacher.

Meditate, stretch, write, run, teach.

I'm changing in small ways. Watching my emotions,
 my environment neater, breaking through—the only
 approval I need is me. Letting up on the world, loved
 ones.

But what about all of them speeding around in their
 cars, the need to compete...meditate, stretch, run,
 write, teach.

If the universe has no boundaries perhaps I should
 relax and let it take care of its kind.

Thinking these thoughts as I take the
 bus ride from the San Francisco airport.

A long complex journey home.

Me in a three piece suit gazing out the window.

See an ordinary man walking on a midday
 average afternoon.

My bus haughtily eases up the street. I'm in
 the world of hotel rooms, taxi fares, assured
 people who make me doubt.

Meditate, looking within—no place
   to go, a bird sound, noises of eternity.

My body isn't even solid, the atoms don't hold
   together.
Being is just an idea, the dirt I clean is what
   I return to.

Looking at you, and you seeing me is only an illusion.

Then how come every personal encounter, decision,
    interaction, puts me through all kinds of changes.

I'm finding that running only delivers me or
   makes me run away, fight or flight. I'm looking
   for a greater discipline to take me homeward.

Meditate, stretch, run, write, teach. The time in
   between is just the waiting for the next activity.

And at least this way, you know you are alive.

Sit down, relax and read a good book...

CURRENT BESTSELLERS FROM BERKLEY

IN 1942 THE U.S. RATIONED GASOLINE

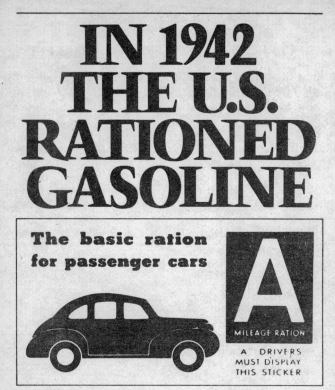

The basic ration for passenger cars

A

MILEAGE RATION

A DRIVERS MUST DISPLAY THIS STICKER

That was wartime and the spirit of sacrifice was in the air. No one liked it, but everyone went along. Today we need a wartime spirit to solve our energy problems. A spirit of thrift in our use of all fuels, especially gasoline. We Americans pump over 200 million gallons of gasoline into our automobiles each day. That is nearly one-third the nation's total daily oil consumption and more than half of the oil we import every day . . . at a cost of some $40 billion a year. So conserving gasoline is more than a way to save money at the pump and help solve the nation's balance of payments; it also can tackle a major portion of the nation's energy problem. And that is something we all have a stake in doing . . . with the wartime spirit, but without the devastation of war or the inconvenience of rationing.

ENERGY CONSERVATION - IT'S YOUR CHANCE TO SAVE, AMERICA

Department of Energy, Washington, D.C.

A PUBLIC SERVICE MESSAGE FROM BERKLEY PUBLISHING CO., INC.